KU-223-523

JOHN SPEDAN LEWIS

1885-1963

Remembered by some of his
contemporaries in the
centenary year of his birth

Acknowledgments

The illustrations in this book are from the John Lewis Partnership archive collection except for the following, for whose inclusion grateful acknowledgment is made: New Lanark Conservation Trust p22; Miss Mary Dunhill p33; Glyndebourne Festival Opera p37 above and below; Her Majesty's Stationery Office p40 above and below (from the 1947 Utility Catalogue); Area Museums Service for South Eastern England and the Geffrye Museum p41 below left; The British Museum of Natural History p103; The Daily Mail p154, p177; Mr Donald Herbert p163 centre right; Magdalen College Archives p210 below; Mr Keith Morris p6, p47, p50, p51, p54 below, p55, p118 above, p125, p126, p160 below, p161, p162, p163 below left and above right, p186 above, p203 above; Mrs Marion Hughes p54 above, p137 above, p178 above, p179 below; Mr Jeremy Bate p80, p81, p121; Mr Trevor Fry p170, p171, p173, p186 below, p192, p197, p200 above.
Map by John Flower p96.

Front cover: a resin bronze bas-relief by Michael Rizello PRBS ARCA
Frontispiece: John Spedan Lewis aged 19

Published in 1985 by the John Lewis Partnership
© John Lewis plc
All rights reserved. No part of this publication may be reproduced, stored in a retrieval system or transmitted in any form or by any means, electronic, mechanical, photocopying, recording or otherwise without the prior permission of John Lewis plc

Editor: Hugh Macpherson
Partnership history: Rosalind Hadden
Indexer: Lorna Poole
Sub-editor: Fiona Pearson
Researcher: Marek Effendowicz
Designer: Paul Watkins

Text filmsetting by
BAS Printers Limited, Over Wallop, Hampshire.
Printed in England by Jolly & Barber Ltd., Rugby.
Bound in Edinburgh by Hunter & Foulis Ltd.

The John Lewis Partnership

The Partnership is a retail business run on co-operative principles. In 1984 sales were £1,206 million and the total capital employed was £334 million.

The business belongs to those who work in it. All except those engaged temporarily are Partners from the day they join, and all the ordinary share capital is held by trustees on their behalf.

Under irrevocable trusts Partners get all the profits, after provision for prudent reserves and for interest on loans and fixed dividends on shares held outside. A large part of the distribution is made direct in the form of Partnership Bonus, shared among Partners at the end of the trading year as a percentage of their pay; for 1984 this amounted to £26 million.

The principal authorities in the Partnership under its written constitution are the Chairman; the Central Council, representing all Partners; and the Central Board (the Board of John Lewis Partnership plc), five of whose twelve directors are elected by the Central Council. A vote by two-thirds of the Central Council that the Chairman was no longer a suitable person to be Chairman would lead to his replacement.

The Partnership aims to run its business efficiently and competitively, and at the same time to enable its members to enjoy full information about it, to express their views freely, to co-operate in shaping its policies and to share in its rewards. Management is accountable to the general body of Partners, in particular through elected Councils and through the Partnership's journalism.

As its Founder wrote, "The Partnership's supreme purpose is to secure the fairest possible sharing by all its members of the advantages of ownership—gain, knowledge and power; that is to say, their happiness in the broadest sense of that word so far as happiness depends upon gainful occupation. No one partnership can hope to suit everyone and the John Lewis Partnership does not attempt to do so. It is intended only for those who to be really happy need to feel they are giving good service to the general community and whom its character and methods suit well enough in all other ways."

Contents

Foreword

Mr P T Lewis, Chairman of the John Lewis Partnership

John Spedan Lewis born 22 September 1885

Few of us celebrate our own centenary and few of us can expect anyone else to celebrate it for us in our absence. But Spedan cannot be forgotten as long as the John Lewis Partnership flourishes. The idea of the Partnership is inseparable from its daily business and Spedan brought his idea to life in such a vivid and personal way that the Founder will always move like a shadow behind the Partnership for as long as it survives. His distinction was that he acted decisively in real life where so many only talk and dream. He was a towering pioneer and the future, I am sure, will increasingly recognise it.

This book is for those who would like a chance to eavesdrop (and who does not?) at a reunion of the diminishing band who knew Spedan personally–a bundle of recollections, a glimpse of the man, published as a token on the 100th anniversary of his birth.

Peter Lewis
22 September 1985

The Founder

JSL in the early 1950s: a portrait by Anthony Devas

Not many men devote their life to a single great cause. This is fortunate for the rest of us, since great causes, or magnificent obsessions, are the hallmark of the political demagogue and the religious fanatic. Fewer still have the personal or material resources to pursue their obsessions, no matter how worthy, to fruition – particularly in the perilous territory where idealism and realism meet. Even rarer is the man whose great cause embodies a system which finally excludes its creator from power. Such a man was John Spedan Lewis.

He was born on 22 September 1885, the son of John Lewis, a West Country draper who had come to London over twenty-one years before, established himself in a small shop in Oxford Street, and prospered. His success enabled Spedan to enter Westminster School, where he was a Queen's Scholar. At the age of 19 he entered his father's business and, when 21, was given £50,000 capital together with a quarter share of the profits of the Oxford Street shop. Shortly afterwards, he was placed on the board of Peter Jones, an ailing store which John Lewis had purchased the year before, in 1905, by putting £20,000 in his pocket and walking from Oxford Street to Sloane Square.*

Early on Spedan became aware of the disparity between the benefits gained from the business by his family and those gained by its employees. The idea of the John Lewis Partnership began to form in his mind. He described some of his youthful reasonings many years later in a broadcast, in 1957, on the BBC West of England Home Service:

"My father, who had been born in Somersetshire, worked his way to London and there in his twenty-ninth year started business for himself in one little shop in Oxford Street. Forty years later, on my own nineteenth birthday, I came into that business. By then it was large but still wholly his own.

It was soon clear to me that my father's success had been due to his trying constantly to give very good value to people who wished to exchange their money for his merchandise; but it also became clear to me that the business would have grown further, and that my father's life would have been much happier, if he had done the same for those who wished to exchange their work for his money.

The profit, even after ten thousand pounds had been set aside as interest at 5 per cent upon the capital, was equal to

* Details of the significant events in Spedan Lewis's life are contained within the Chronology of the Partnership in the latter half of this book.

the whole of the pay of the staff, of whom there were about three hundred.

To his two children my father seemed to have all that anyone could want. Yet for years he had been spending no more than a small fraction of his income. On the other hand, for very nearly all of his staff any saving worth mentioning was impossible. They were getting hardly more than a bare living. The pay-sheet was small even for those days.

The ideas, in this respect, that my father followed with the exceptional ability and energy that he put into all of his work, were not surprising in someone whose start in life had been so different from that which his hard-won success had enabled him to give to his two sons. But six years of contact with the results of those ideas led me to the notion of the John Lewis Partnership, the notion that the relation of employers to employees should be that of lawyers or stockbrokers to their clients, or of doctors to their patients, or of teachers and trainers to their students. None of these experts ask for their services more than a definite fee quite moderate in relation to the importance of the service they give for it. Beyond that fixed amount the whole of the benefit goes to the client or patient or pupil."

What Spedan Lewis did not explain was *why* he became so determined to distribute wealth and power among those who worked for him. As early as 1920 he was dismissive of some of the more obvious motives, in a piece he wrote for *The Gazette* on the powers of the Chairman:

"It is natural for people to be unable really to believe that the true ultimate motives of another person can be different from those familiar to their own minds and they are apt to regard the possible motives in such a case as limited to one of four –

Religious Belief/Appetite for Money/or Power/or Social Distinction

In the case we are considering there seem to be none of the ordinary signs of exceptional religious views. Heads of Businesses have been known to exert themselves to create, or to confirm among those who worked under them, a particular religious belief or particular religious practices. The Partners see that I do nothing in that way and Religious Motive therefore does not occur to them as a possible explanation of my system.

Appetite for Money, the commonest and in this country the nearly universal motive of independent Business Authorities, seems to them to be likewise pretty well ruled out by the fact that I have declared my intention of giving to those, who work in the Business, the whole of its true profits and that up to the present time I have been as good as my word and have even gone further and given up last year's Ordinary Dividend and my personal salary for that year. The Money motive, therefore, does not seem to them to be available as an explanation.

The last possibility – Appetite for Social Distinction – would obviously come so much more easily from a legal or a political career that it probably does not occur to their minds at all, any more than does the first possibility, and they are therefore left with the idea of Appetite for Personal Power as the only possible explanation consistent with their own normal ideas and long-established habits of mind.

It does not occur to them that there may be people who will devote themselves to the invention of a new system of business for its own sake exactly as a man may devote himself to scientific research or to writing a book or to painting a picture, simply for the sake of doing the thing and not for any consequential reward at all."

Whatever the immediate personal fascination in creating a partnership, it is surely significant that he came to early manhood at a time of great political change in Britain and abroad. The old security of the imperialist 19th century was being replaced by the liberalism of the 20th and the extension of parliamentary democracy in some parts of Europe including Britain.

While Spedan was at Westminster School, the Marquess of Salisbury formed the last great aristocratic administration in 1895. Even as he was being made a part-owner of his father's business at the age of twenty-one, the celebrated Liberal government of 1906, with glittering figures like Lloyd George, Asquith and Churchill, was taking office and the newly formed Labour party appeared with thirty seats.

As a young man he could hardly have escaped that heady climate of democratic change. Beyond that it is difficult to trace any particular influence. Perhaps it happened at Westminster School. Perhaps the fact that the party leading social change was that of his father (who was a Liberal Councillor even as Campbell-Bannerman formed his 1906 government) had an influence on him. In the final analysis he is an example of the sterility of the question as to whether great men make history, or history makes great men. Great men are those rare creatures of vision who seize the currents of history. In a minor way that is what he was.

For more than forty years he devoted his extraordinary energies to creating the Partnership. Starting in Peter Jones, as early as 1915, he established the first element in the extensive partnership system of democracy – the Committees for Communication which still function today. In 1950 he signed an irrevocable Trust Settlement (twenty-one years after signing the first one) which transferred the annual profits of the Partnership to those employed within it and allowed the capital to be held in trust by the elected Trustees of the Constitution.

During those years he showed almost immeasurable resolve in the face of opposition from bankers, shareholders, his own father, and sometimes even the people to whom he was giving so much. There were periods of dire economic difficulty which made the future precarious.

When times became difficult he did not hesitate to sell his home and estate in Harrow to move into an apartment, refuse his salary, and even sell off some of his investments to keep the Partnership going.

Apart from the high economic cost there were other prices to be paid. He referred to this in answering a churlish letter to *The Gazette* just at the point when he was signing away his power, in 1950. The anonymous correspondent "Lumper" accused him of keeping down wages and raising the price of meals.

In reply Spedan Lewis pointed out that in pre-war days Partners gained from him, in the prices of that day, more than half a million pounds, and after the 1939–45 war at least another £800,000. In addition there was a pension fund which stood, then, at more than a million and a quarter pounds. He continued:

"My business-career began on my nineteenth birthday. Next September I shall be sixty-five. Through all these forty-six years I have had so little holiday that I have travelled hardly at all in Europe and never anywhere else and my work has left me hardly any leisure for making friends or for any other interests outside the Partnership.

The war has now reduced very greatly the value of the money in which the Partnership will be paying out the remainder of my capital. Nevertheless, I am on the point of making to the Partners present and future an irrevocable gift of the whole of the Deferred Ordinary Shares in John Lewis Partnership Ltd . . . They carry the control of the business that I have spent my life in building upon the foundations that my father spent his life in creating . . .

If I make this gift to the Partners present and future, I shall be doing so in the teeth of strong advice from an experienced lawyer and from some other friends . . . A main part of their argument is that the Partnership contains too many people with minds like 'Lumper's'."

Certainly the opportunities lost for a man of his intelligence and energies were considerable. There is little doubt that he would have enjoyed a distinguished career at the Bar. He was an amateur naturalist of considerable ability, interested in the classics, a keen chess player, a supporter of Glyndebourne, and an intrepid, if not particularly gifted, sportsman. He might even have made a politician but for the fact that he would probably have insisted that he become prime minister at the outset which, in the nature of our political life, would have been difficult.

And that was a flaw in his character – for he was no saintly figure labouring in a self–effacing manner but could be autocratic and quixotic in his judgments. Indeed it is clear that there was a curious contradiction between his altruism in creating the Partnership, together with great personal kindness, and his behaviour at times towards those who worked most closely for him. The preface to *Retail Trading*, a collection of his exhilarating memoranda, privately published in 1968, contains this passage:

"It is hard to be objective about a man to whom as much is owed as Partners owe to Spedan Lewis. But we ought to try. The Partnership has sometimes been accused of swallowing gladly an overdose of ancestor worship. There is no need at all for this and it does the Founder of the Partnership no true service. We ought to be able to admit that he was vain and cantankerous, and it would not be hard to demonstrate that he was intolerant and sometimes cruel in the intellectual arrogance with which he treated individuals who were his mental inferiors. In some ways he was a humbug and he certainly sacrificed his family to his dream of partnership. In the last quarter of his life he was impossibly verbose and at the end when the remorseless requirement of his dream demanded that he should give up power and he did it, his human frailty was such that he could not accept all the consequences. We can recognise these things without ingratitude because none of them diminishes what Spedan Lewis accomplished.''

However, that part of his nature is heavily outweighed by his achievements, not the least of which was his insistence that the Partnership system be drawn so tightly, legally, that it was proof against interference even from himself once he retired. This proved distressingly necessary: for such a fiery man was simply not made to go quietly into the night.

After his retirement he severely criticised his successors, often through the anonymous letters system in *The Gazette*, in sulphurous missives which were instantly recognisable..It placed great stress, particularly on his successor, Sir Bernard Miller, who bore it all with almost superhuman restraint.

Although this was admirable, it was hardly surprising, for yet another of Spedan Lewis's inspirations was to surround himself with men and women of high academic ability and great personal integrity. Of course he recruited them in a buyer's market in labour, during the twenties and thirties, and he paid well. But their attachment to him owed most to his personal charisma and purposes. His retirement years may have been as tempestuous, if more negative, than his industrious prime but the respect and affection in which he was held by his heirs was undiminished. They built on his secure foundations.

To celebrate the centenary of his birth I went to see some of the men and women who worked close to him and asked them for their personal memories. A few of the contributions are, alas, posthumous.

For those who are unfamiliar with the history of the Partnership there is an illustrated chronology prepared by the Editor of *The Gazette*, Miss Rosalind Hadden, and by the Archivist, Mrs Lorna Poole.

What appears is not intended to be a balanced, let alone a definitive, study of the Founder. It is a series of personal pictures of an extraordinary man, whose greatest monument lies in the successful business the Partnership has become while adhering to, and extending, the democratic system which he created.

Hugh Macpherson General Editor

WILLIAM LEWIS
of Shepton Mallet

MICHAEL LEWIS=AMY
of Shepton Mallet
born c 1710
buried 22.2.1766

[it is possible that William and
Michael were grandsons of a
GEORGE LEWIS who paid hearth tax
at West Pennard in 1664/5]

8 children
the sixth of which was
GEORGE LEWIS of Shepton Mallet=ELIZABETH CHAMPION of Shepton Mallet
bapt. 7.2.1740
buried 16.4.1803
aged 62

4 children
the third of which was
NEHEMIAH LEWIS of Cowl Street=ELIZABETH HARNIMAN of Shepton Mallet
Shepton Mallet
b c 1768 but not
baptised until 1777
buried 5.3.1818

JOHN LEWIS
of Town Street Shepton Mallet=ELIZABETH SPEED
Cabinet maker and baker
b 1798 bapt 1799
married in Shepton Mallet
17.12.1824
died 12.4.1843

from a long-established
Shepton Mallet family
daughter of
William Speed of Shepton Mallet
one of her sisters was the
ANNE SPEED often mentioned

and eight other children
SAMUEL
HENRY
ELIZABETH
JAMES
WILLIAM (I) died in infancy
MARY ANN
MARIA
WILLIAM (II)

JOHN LEWIS
b 24.2.1836 in Shepton Mallet=ELIZA BAKER
bapt. 14.8.1836
in the Hepzibah Chapel
later silk mercer and draper
and founder of the Oxford
Street store which still
carries his name
d 19.9.1928

on 1.11.1884
at Stoke Bishop
in Gloucestershire

ELIZABETH (I) died in infancy
MARY
ANNE
MARIA
ELIZABETH (II)

JOHN SPEDAN LEWIS
creator of the John
Lewis Partnership
b 22.9.1885
d 21.2.1963

OSWALD LEWIS
b 5.4.1887
d 12.2.1966

Extract from the
Lewis Family Tree

Spedan and Oswald Lewis with their mother, c 1895

Spedan Lewis, c 1904

Oswald Lewis in the uniform of an officer
in the Westminster Dragoons, 1914

Spedan as a boy, c 1896

Spedan in Westminster School academic dress

Spedan Lewis (aged 17) with his mother and two of her friends, 1902

Climbing onto a wreck. Spedan on holiday in Ireland, 1903

John Lewis in 1910

John Lewis at Spedan Tower on his 91st birthday

Three generations of John Lewises: Spedan with his father and his son in 1924

John Lewis three weeks before his death. Spedan Tower garden, 28 May 1928

John Spedan Lewis married Sarah Beatrice Mary Hunter in 1923.
This portrait of her by John St Helier Lander was
commissioned by Oswald Lewis as a wedding present

Sir Bernard Miller

Sir Bernard Miller succeeded John Spedan Lewis to become the Partnership's second Chairman in 1955. (From that time Spedan Lewis was referred to as "The Founder".) He came to the Partnership with a first in history from Jesus College, Oxford, in 1927. Now he is one of the few who remember John Lewis, the Founder's father, visiting the Oxford Street shop.

Sir Bernard's career was mainly on the financial side in the Partnership and outside, where he served on the Monopolies Commission and was a Tax Commissioner. In recognition of his many public services, he was knighted in 1967. Under his Chairmanship the Partnership flourished and expanded, as can be traced in the brief history on page 138.

Upon his retirement, in 1972, he vigorously pursued his public activities, becoming honorary Treasurer of the council of Southampton University which conferred a doctorate of law on him in 1981, and elected him Pro-Chancellor in January 1983. He continues to champion music and the arts as he did during his Chairmanship. Sir Bernard and Lady Miller live in Longstock. Two of his three sons are in senior management in the Partnership.

Further biographical details are to be found on page 215.

Do you remember your first meeting with the Founder?

I remember it vividly. I saw him in his office. He had a very high desk in those days and all one could see of him, initially, was his face and shoulders. I should describe him as having a very long chin, a long body, shortish legs, a very impressive face and tremendous dynamism. He was a very handsome man, very fastidious in his personal appearance – indeed, in everything he did. He'd be impeccably dressed, his hands would be beautifully maintained and his hair would be cut once a week – he aimed at perfection in his own turnout, just as he did in everything else. He was the sort of chap romantic novelists try to describe, but he was much more than just a handsome and impressive man. He seemed to be almost on the point of explosion all the time, tremendous force coming out of this very long chin. The absolute dynamism of the man came through. One knew he was somebody really out of this world.

I hadn't any intention of going into business but I was so swept away by him that I forgot all about the other things I had in mind. I had taken the Civil Service examination and got a place. I had also already got myself a job as a senior history master at Dover College – I was a "belt and braces" man, as you may well have gathered. But after I had talked to Spedan I was quite happy to have a go. We talked about his Partnership ideas and something about the intention of the business, about which of course I knew nothing, but he was so completely convincing that I finally said yes.

What did he offer you that attracted you?

It wasn't any particular job; it was a chance to play a part in this idea of his. He said he was recruiting from universities to get people to form a team to develop the Partnership. He engaged me as a trainee with, I think, a clear view that I should move up fairly fast.

Was it then that you were attracted to the idea of Partnership as such?

No, but I had a background because, as part of my finals, I did "Economic History in the 19th Century" and I was very much taken with the Owenite experiment and trade union relations. This sort of triggered it off in my mind. I wouldn't claim that I was an apostle of the Partnership and that this was what I had come for, but it was something that clicked into place.

Overleaf: The Strathclyde village of New Lanark which the 19th century reformer Robert Owen sought to transform into a model of industrial and social efficiency

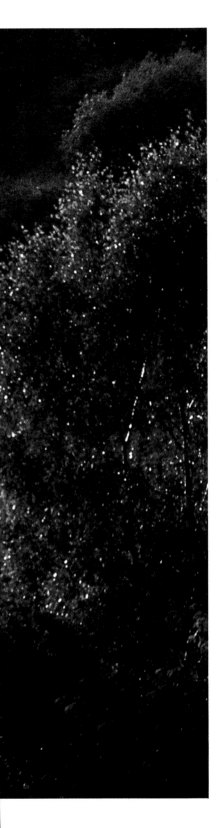

He made me feel it wasn't just a question of making money but that he had ideas which were really a 20th century manifestation of the sort of thing that had been stirring in the early part of the 19th.

One never felt one was running a lot of wage earners; one was part of a team, and everybody recognised that some had to manage and some had to be managed. This was what Spedan spent all his time drumming into people right from the start.

I think he was very successful in those days. Of course the Partnership was much smaller then, and everybody knew him.

So he knew everyone?

I wouldn't say he knew everyone but they knew him and he talked with everyone. If anyone wrote to him about anything he would write back as though he knew them personally. He might put them firmly in their place but they didn't feel they were part of a machine which was using them to make a lot of money.

Was he still under the shadow of his father at that time?

For the first six months or so that I knew him, yes, he was. His father still came down from Hampstead in the old Rolls Royce from time to time and would sweep around the place sacking anybody he didn't like the look of. The word would go round: "Old John's coming in, so make yourself scarce".

After the old man died Spedan was entirely free and that's why the Partnership's Constitution, the formalisation of the Partnership's structure, started in 1929.

Did you see changes in him when he suddenly found himself in sole command?

I wasn't really working closely enough with him to do that. I was in the silk department for quite a long time and then, when they found out I was colour blind, they took me out of silks and put me on to doing secretarial work for Michael Watkins [Sir Metford Watkins]. So I wasn't in such close contact with Spedan in the way that I was when I became his personal assistant. That really was a hectic period.

What was a typical day like when you were his assistant?

I don't know about a typical day. I can remember several occasions when I would work all morning and then go out to lunch

at North Hall where he lived. But I had to have my notebook with me because work went on over lunch, so I didn't get much to eat.

On other occasions one would work until after everybody had gone. Then about 7.30 he'd say "We'll just go and have some dinner" and we'd go up to a fish place, Prunier, in Regent Street. You'd be driven almost to the point of desperation by the rate at which he worked, then he'd suddenly put you right with a jolly good meal.

It was very hard work because he was in the middle of organising the Partnership, working it out in his own mind as he went along. Although he dictated a lot of memoranda to his secretaries, when he was trying to formulate something, he involved me, and I had to produce notes and memos afterwards. But it was all very exciting. At times one thought this man must be crazy, but one was swept along. It was really a tremendous experience.

Can you tell me about his relationship with the other brilliant group of men he had around him, people like Sir Metford Watkins?

Well, because he was an outstanding dialectician his debating power was enormous. Although Michael Watkins was a very intelligent man and a very good debater, Spedan could out-argue him, and I think Michael probably often found himself agreeing with Spedan against his better judgment.

Of course, Michael himself was outstanding. There was nobody else like him in the Partnership. The rest of the people, at my sort of level, were – it sounds immodest to say it – no better than me, so Spedan didn't have much difficulty in impressing his views and philosophy on them.

There were a lot of service people – I'm speaking now of the period 1928–30. They were very good, very able, and very conscientious, but they did not have deep-thinking minds. There was also a large graduate intake, but some of it wasn't of very high quality.

He got a lot of people in from the Indian Civil Service who were pretty high-powered intellectuals, but they didn't last; they couldn't take it. I didn't look on them as particularly brilliant people but they must have been high-powered because of the positions they had achieved in Indian government. But I wasn't surprised when they dropped out.

If they dropped out and couldn't take it, why did men like Sir Metford Watkins and yourself put up with it?

Because one felt that the end was greater than the means. One felt one was being pushed around a bit but that the whole thing was worth it and that he was, in fact, putting everything he'd got into it. As he'd got much more than anybody else, one had to respect that and say "All right, we'll go along with this, warts and all".

How well did he take to people standing up to him?

It depended who they were. He took quite well to Paul May, though there was a point at which he wouldn't be pushed even though he was wrong, no matter who it was. By and large, anybody he didn't respect who stood up to him got a very raw deal indeed. The arguments pursuing something were very convincing if you left out the human factor, but he didn't want to concede too much to the fact that it was human to err and

so on. There was a whole range of shades of opposition but when anyone who had a case, and whose judgment and ability he respected, stood up to him, he'd say all right, have you thought what you're going to do?

Who would you regard, then, as the influential men about him in the period from 1927 to the start of war in 1939?

Michael Watkins first of all. There was Cecil Hunter, Mrs Lewis's cousin, who had been General Manager of the Sudan Railways and who came in as corresponding to what is now Director of Trading. He and Spedan crossed swords quite a bit and eventually, when Cecil Hunter was offered the top job in the Sudan Railways, he went back and finished his career out there.

But there was a series of people: Sir Algernon Peyton, who was a most unlikely draper but a very sound man. He did a variety of jobs – General Inspector, Managing Director of Peter Jones, and so on – he was a great influence on Spedan who respected his views quite a lot. Then there were two or three very experienced and able buying people whom he got in from Harrods, and other places, whose judgment he respected.

There were three textile buyers, Hughes, Ledbrooke and Thomas – Thomas was a big extrovert man who used to sweep round Europe buying silks. Those three were very important influences on the trading side. Max Baker was steadily making his mark in the thirties on the merchandising side; Donald Radermacher, who was an old Westminster boy, was General Manager of Oxford Street, or various parts of it, from time to time. He was a very sound man and Spedan relied on him a lot on the trading side. For the others there was a series of fairly high-powered people who came and went and didn't have any lasting influence on the development of the Partnership.

One man who did play a very important part was John Moss, who was Counting House Manager at Oxford Street. He knew the trade inside out and he'd been old John's right-hand man at Oxford Street for years.

The other man, of course, was Sebastian Earl, who was very distinguished. He played an important part in running the selling side and he was General Inspector for a time – everybody did different jobs while the thing was being worked out and we all had various titles. It was all a gradual crystallisation. I think really you can say that Sebastian Earl and Michael Watkins

Sir Bernard Miller, 1984. A portrait by John Whittall to mark Sir Bernard's 80th birthday

were the important ones. I wasn't really a force in the land until the war came along. Then, of course, everybody else went off and I monitored their jobs.

It's interesting that he employed so many bright men. What were his own intellectual abilities?

Very high indeed. He reminds me very much of Enoch Powell, with that same capacity for developing a convincing argument and pursuing it to its conclusions in a way that a lot of people don't: they start by rationalising but when it seems to lead to a conclusion that doesn't fit, they drop it. Spedan didn't do that. He would think a thing right through and would base his action on that.

He was tremendously widely read, with a talent for amassing knowledge from a wide variety of fields. So he was always able to find parallels and similes to illustrate a point.

If one were to criticise his intellectual capacity, it would be to say that in individual cases the human factor seemed to be ignored entirely, which was strange because, in dealing with people in the mass, his humanity was superabundantly evident. He really did care for people. He wanted to help and the examples of his helping individual people, both inside and outside the Partnership, without anyone knowing about it, were innumerable. So one can't accuse him of inhumanity. I think it just was a demand on human efficiency, on human avoidance of failure, that was too highly developed for some people. That led some people to question his intellectual ability because they couldn't go along with his conclusions. He could find the weak points in anyone else's argument with tremendous accuracy and devastating pungency, which made him a formidable debating opponent.

He did, however, make some major mistakes. One I can remember was just before the Korean war when prices went sky high. There was tremendous inflation for 12 months or so, then it dropped with a resounding bang in the following 12 months. The Partnership lost a lot of money in that period. We had built up rather high stocks when prices were still rising. Michael Watkins and I both thought we were taking too much of a risk and ought to mark the stuff down to get rid of it.

Spedan wouldn't have it. He said we were throwing money away and that if it was good stock we would dispose of it. He proved to be wrong. Prices crashed in the following spring and

28

Opposite: Notes made by JSL in 1918 showing the degree of detail with which he planned the projected profit-sharing scheme

we were left with a packet of stock. As we were producers as well as retailers – this was mainly in the textiles field, where we had heavy commitments in the production end as well – we had to mark down our own stuff to get rid of it. Our competitors, who hadn't gone into production and hadn't got any stock, took advantage of the fact that the producers were up against it and sold at prices vastly below ours. We couldn't allow that, so we had to reduce ours and consequently lost a lot on it. That was one case in which Spedan argued from first principles and it proved to be completely wrong.

Did he acknowledge he was wrong?

No. That's one of the things he didn't do. He didn't take kindly to admitting he'd made a mistake. He would, in fact, take it to heart and his future actions would be clearly influenced by the recognition that he had been wrong. In that particular case his recognition was more or less to opt out of merchandising altogether. Although he was still Chairman, and I was Deputy Chairman, he handed everything over to me and told me to reorganise it. That was when we reorganised the buying side, cut out a lot of Directors of Buying and simplified the buying structure. I'm quite sure that was because he'd realised it wasn't working properly.

If he didn't take the blame then, did anyone have to pay the price?

No. He wouldn't acknowledge that it was his mistake but he wouldn't deliberately try to unload the blame onto someone else if he thought it wasn't justified. If he thought it *was* justified – and in most cases he did think it was justified – he unloaded it very heavily indeed, and you paid the price. He mellowed in his later years so that he was able to say: "You were a bloody fool over this but no doubt you'll learn for the future", whereas ten or 15 years earlier you would have been out.

Was he a good retailer, or was he simply a man who was very good at getting other people to do it?

I think his prime contribution, in Partnership terms, was in building up a big and successful retailing structure, but he was a superb retailer as an individual shopkeeper. There were many occasions when he went out and bought things that were a complete success. On other occasions he bought things, marked them very cheaply, but they didn't sell. He would then say:

"We probably marked them too cheaply", upped the price and sold the lot. He had that sort of flair for retailing.

His management of stock was probably better than that of anyone else in the retailing trade at that time, in the sense that he set up systems to monitor what was happening to stock. He knew the winners and the losers, and acted accordingly. He discontinued lines and would mark down things to get rid of them before it was too late.

I have no doubt whatever that had he started out in life as his father did, trying to make a business, he would have been just as successful. It would have been on rather different lines but he would have made a business. Having said that, I think, in respect of both the Partnership and retailing on a large scale, he was really more interested in building up the structure than in operating it once he'd got it. He was apt to lose interest when he'd got something that was working. His eyes really sparkled when he said "We've got to devise a new structure for buying", or "Let's reorganise the central administration of this, that or the other".

In the early 1930s, when he was still crystallising his mind and the ideas of the Partnership, and getting ready to write his books, that was when he was at his best in theorising, working out ideas and seeing how they meshed together.

He was enormously good at detail. He could devise some particular plan on quite a large scale and carry it down to the minutest detail of how it was to operate. That, I'm sure, is what really sparked him off and where he got the greatest pleasure. He could carry a lot of detail in his own mind, but as the thing got larger, he wasn't really interested in running an administrative machine. He was certainly interested in sitting at the top and seeing the results, but he wouldn't have got the pleasure that a chap like Max Baker, for example, or Paul May, would have done in making sure the machine really did its stuff, guiding it gently this way and that.

In the period up to the war a lot of people seemed to come and go.

Yes, you're right. It was a formative period when a lot of people came and went, but one must remember the Partnership was expanding all the time. From 1933 onwards we started on the branches. Peter Jones was rebuilding, John Lewis was rebuilding, so he had to recruit extra people. We had a lot of amusing

John Lewis, Oxford Street:
the rebuilt Cavendish Square
section, 1938

people about the place in the early days. It was all great fun and it didn't matter very much that most of them weren't much good. Later on, of course, it did matter, and gradually our recruiting was directed more towards getting good people from other firms. We still went on recruiting from Oxford and Cambridge – they were almost the only universities he recognised.

The Partnership in those days was a complicated structure so far as management was concerned. Management was a difficult job. It's even more difficult now but we have at least structured and rationalised it a bit so that we can recognise the burdens and provide for them to be carried. But in those days they were all carried by people in management. So that was an additional factor in making many people leave.

You were getting closer to him at this stage?

Yes. I worked very closely with him, particularly during the war, and indeed from the 1930s onwards. I became Company Secretary in 1931 and that was when I really came into the inner councils.

The Byron cricket team, c 1906.
JSL middle row, third from left,
wearing large hat

One way and another, my wife and I did see a lot of him on a personal basis. We used to play tennis with him at North Hall in Hampstead before we were married and we'd have some very keen tennis matches. He had a tennis court made with cages at each end in which he kept lynxes. One of these cages was up against the back netting, so if you went to pick up your ball, there was a lynx about a foot away. It was quite extraordinary but that was typical of him – he loved wild animals.

We used to go on skiing holidays with the Lewises in the early 1930s. They'd go for a month at a time and people would come out and stay for about a fortnight. The holidays were very good value and it brought together a lot of people who were then gradually building up as a team inside the Partnership. Jack Webster went several times and Spedan also used to take his secretaries. Constance Lynn and Muriel Elliott would go, and another of Mrs Lewis's cousins, John Hunter, and his wife.

What form did these ski trips take?

Well, we'd go out as a party. Spedan was very keen on skiing but he wasn't any good and would get very exasperated. He used to hire a professional to come and stay with us, a chap

Thatched Holme, one of the properties at Wargrave that JSL bought for his wife in 1926

called Caulfield who was then the outstanding ski coach in this country. He was an ex-British champion and he'd take charge of the parties and have various classes graded according to ability.

Michael Watkins always came. He was very keen, a bit of a wild skier but great fun. And various women from the Partnership came too. It was a successful mixing together of a lot of the people whom Spedan had recruited with a view to their playing a part in the Partnership. In that way he could see what you were really like, because you can't keep up any sort of pretence for a fortnight. You are as you are when you get out on the ski slopes.

What sort of sportsman was he generally?

He was very keen on tennis and played a lot. He had an absolutely devastating forehand drive. He always ran round the ball but when it worked it swept you right off the court. His service wasn't very good and he never attempted to volley. He used to play every morning with his chauffeur, who had to be taught tennis so that he could play with him. He didn't like losing.

He played a lot of cricket too – he wasn't a very good cricketer

and one had to be prepared to make some sort of concessions, but he stuck to it and liked to play.

He bought a house at Wargrave in 1926 and had a tennis court there, so I used to go down at weekends to play. Mrs Oswald Lewis (the present Chairman's mother) was a very good tennis player and we'd have foursomes of various kinds. In the earlier days we had matches and Spedan used to play in those at Cookham with Donald Radermacher and three or four others.

Chess was his main love, I think. He was quite a useful player. When he was having an on-day he was quite difficult to beat. He and I played a lot of chess and we were just about of a kind – if we played 100 matches I would expect to win by 55 to 45 or something like that. He sometimes got angry when something materialised that he hadn't seen – if I pinched his queen or something – that would really upset him.

Did you ever lose to make him happy?

Well, once or twice, when I knew he'd been working hard and was getting a bit uptight. But I really didn't have to. He could beat me as often as I could beat him.

I think he also played snooker and billiards?

Yes, he did. He wasn't a very good player, but he kept going and it was a lot of fun. We used to play Russian pool a lot on the billiard table. None of us was very good, but he wasn't hopeless by any means. He worked so hard at all games and put so much effort into them.

What about the arts? Did you go to the theatre with him at all?

Not very much. But we went to Glyndebourne a lot with him at the time when it first started. He used to take parties of eight or ten. Once or twice he took a house at Seaford for a week and had seats for most of the operas. He was intensely interested in opera, but chamber music was his real love. He bought an enormous number of records. I don't think he went to many concerts.

We did, as you know, start having concerts within the Partnership and he hired chamber orchestras to play at Leckford Abbas or Longstock House towards the end of his time there. I think he used to go to the theatre a bit but I don't think it was a major interest.

JSL playing chess in the Bognor Regis competition, 1955. He tied for first prize

JSL and his wife at Glyndebourne.
Courtesy of the 'Tatler' 1950
Opposite: Glyndebourne
programmes, including the one
for 1969 designed by Osbert
Lancaster.
During the thirties, JSL bought
200 seats for every Glyndebourne
season for use by Partners. It was
his financial guarantee against
loss for the 1950 season which
enabled John Christie, the
founder of Glyndebourne, to
restart full scale post-war
productions

Among those listening to "Seraglio" on the opening night were these four members of the cast of the opera next to be produced, "Cosi Fan Tutte." They were Erich Kunz, Sena Jurinac, Blanda Thebom and Mario Boriello, here walking in the beautiful grounds between acts

AFTER A DECADE—MOZART AT GLYNDEBOURNE AGAIN

Some of the audience who listened to "Seraglio" in a country-house setting on the Sussex Downs

Mr. John Spedan Lewis in conversation with Miss M. Glasgow, General Secretary of the Arts Council of Great Britain

Viscount Esher, chairman of the Old Vic Governors, with Lady Alexandra Howard-Johnston, sister of Earl Haig

Carl Ebert, whose brilliant production of the opera was greatly admired, at table with Lady Esher

Swaebe

Mr. John Christie, founder of Glyndebourne and builder of the opera house, with Mrs. Spedan Lewis

Sir Bernard Miller in 1950

How did he react to wartime conditions?

Well, he had foreseen the possibility of war several years before and had made a start with the branches, not primarily because of the war but as a dispersion of activities. From about the beginning of 1937 we put a lot of effort into air raid precautions, getting everything organised as far as we could. We had complete copies of our sales ledger records sent down to Clearings so that when John Lewis was in fact bombed and we lost all our records, we had duplicate sets. We didn't have corresponding sets of our liabilities to creditors, such as stock purchases, so we had to ask people to send in their applications and say what they thought we owed them.

Did the war change his attitude to management?

It had to a bit because we'd recruited extensively from the services–the Army and Navy in particular–and of course as soon as the war broke out the whole of our management disappeared overnight. I was nominated to carry the torch at home and more or less told to stay there. Well, I'm not a hero but it was a bit tiresome at times.

On top of that, soon after the war started, the Board of Trade, as it then was, asked Michael Watkins to come and organise the Utility Scheme, the rationing of clothing and so on, which he did with extraordinary success – that was what he got his knighthood for – so we really were battling along while the others were away.

A lot of those service chaps came back after the war, but our recruiting seemed to take a different turn. We had two sweeps, which were probably a product of the war. I think Spedan woke up to the fact that we were short on potential top management. He'd had four people in mind for this in the 1930s: Michael Watkins, Seb Earl, Tom Robinson, and myself. Watkins killed himself in the war with overwork, and Earl and Robinson broke down in health. Spedan realised how risky our preparations for management succession were and, as a result, in 1945, and again in 1955, we had a sweep round outside to get in some really top level people.

Was he involved in this kind of recruitment?

Very much so. I vetted the applications and he did the interviews. He was directly involved in that right up until he retired. It was something he was good at, and was one of the causes

38

of reproach to me that I didn't keep it up. He didn't realise that after you'd got in half a dozen top level chaps you'd got to give them a bit of air – it's no use crowding them with another half dozen on their heels three years later – which is one of the reasons he thought I was doing such a poor job and kept on at me. One can see his argument that you can't have too many good people. Well, you *can* have too many. If there are too many ready for one job when it turns up, you put one in and you lose the others.

What other road was he taking in the period after the war?

Almost entirely writing the philosophy of the Partnership, and refining its Constitution, which wasn't finally settled until the Second Settlement of 1950. That occupied the whole of his attention.

What was your relationship with him after the war?

Much better than it had ever been, because at that stage he regarded himself as having given up the day to day direction of the Partnership. I used to come down and see him regularly to spend the day discussing things. I'd talk about the pay sheet, policy and so on. He still had the final say but he didn't attend meetings of policy, finance or anything like that. I conducted these gatherings. The relationship then was, more or less, of Chairman and Managing Director. He'd look at policy, take an overview of everything while I, broadly speaking, ran the place. That went on until 1955 and our relations then were very good indeed. I felt closer to him than I ever had and he was committed to me by then.

Had he changed in any way from before the war?

Yes, I think he had. He was desperately anxious to get on with his plans up to, and during, the war and couldn't bear to let anything slip or to waste a moment. By 1950, or even earlier, he'd done most of the groundwork of the Partnership, which he was refining, and he was preparing his book. He felt the Partnership was on its way, and that if he died tomorrow it was all right. He lost that sense of intense urgency, although he still had the stimulation of wanting everyone to get on with the job, criticising people if they wasted time and so on. I sensed that he then had the feeling, "Well, I've done the vital job, now I can furnish the fabric that I've constructed".

DINING CHAIRS

DINING CHAIRS

Cotswold Range.
1—Model No. 750 in Oak. Covering : seat in leather cloth.
Model No. 751 in Mahogany. Covering : seat in leather cloth.

2—Model No. 756 in Oak. Covering : seat in leather cloth.

3—Model No. 754 in Oak. Covering : seat and back in leather cloth.

4—Model No. 752 in Oak. Covering : seat and back in leather cloth.
Model No. 753 in Mahogany. Covering : seat and back in leather cloth.

Chiltern Range.
5—Model No. 3 in Oak. Covering : leather cloth.

6—Model No. 3c in Oak. Covering : leather cloth.

7—Model No. 3a in Oak. Covering : leather cloth.

DINING TABLE

Chiltern Range
Top 3 ft. 6 ins. by 2 ft. 6 ins. opening to 5 ft. 6 ins. by 2 ft. 6 ins.
2 ft. 6 ins. high.
Model No. 604 in Oak.

Sir Metford Watkins received his knighthood for work on wartime utility and rationing schemes

HOW TO APPLY

You will need an official permit before you can buy any piece of utility furniture other than nursery furniture, woven fibre furniture or kitchen cabinet. You can collect an application form (UFD/IA) from your Local Fuel Office or obtain one by writing to the Board of Trade, 25 Victoria Street, London, S.W.I, but your claim will be considered only if you are in the priority classes set out on page I of the application form. The applications are considered at the Utility Furniture Office, Board of Trade, Kingsway, Southport, Lancs, and the form is addressed to the office to which it should be sent when completed.

4I

TILITY
URNITURE
AND
ASHION
41—1951

AN EXHIBITION ORIGINALLY COMPILED
E GEFFRYE MUSEUM LONDON E2
CULATING EXHIBITION FROM THE
EUMS SERVICE FOR SOUTH EASTERN ENGLAND

POTATOES

Grade A means—Golden Wonder, King Edward, Red King, Gladstone, Kerr's Pink, Redskin, Arran Victory.

Grade B means—any other variety.

For Potatoes sold in following Districts.	Maximum Wholesale Prices to Retailers, including cost or use of sacks and usual free delivery.	Maximum Retail Prices.			
		Rate per cwt.	Rate per 14 lb. for an amount less than 1 cwt.	Rate per 7 lb. for an amount less than 14 lb.	Rate per 3½ lb. for an amount less than 7 lb.
	per cwt. s. d.	s. d.	s. d.	s. d.	s. d.
Kent ; Surrey ; Sussex ;					
Grade A	9 3	11 3	1 6	9½	5
Grade B	8 3	10 3	1 5	9	4½
Berks, Bucks, Essex (the places marked ; below) : **Herts, London Postal District ; Middlesex ;**					
Grade A	9 0	11 0	1 6	9½	5
Grade B	8 0	9 9	1 5	9	4½
Bedfordshire ; Cambridgeshire (excluding Ely) ; **Essex** (excluding places marked * below) :—					
Grade A	8 9	10 9	1 6	9½	5
Grade B	7 9	9 9	1 5	9	4½

* The Boroughs of Barking and Ilford and the urban districts of Chigwell, Dagenham and Waltham Holy Cross.

Varying prices are prescribed for districts other than those above.

RATIONED FOODS

BACON and **HAM** (except Chaps or Crawls, fore-leg knuckles, hind-leg knuckles and that marked "Free of Ration" above) ; **BUTTER** and **SUGAR** (all varieties including Icing, Barbados, and speciality Castors) are rationed. The amounts of the rations are ½—

	Adult Civilian R.B.1 per week. ozs.	Child R.B.2 per week. ozs.	Travellers R.B.3 per week. ozs.	Seamen R.B.6 per week. ozs.	H.M. Forces, Leave or Duty	
					R.B.8 per week. ozs.	R.B.8a per 3 days. ozs.
Bacon and Ham	8	8	8	8	14	7
					7 ozs. per coupon	
Butter	4	4	4	12	7	3½
					3½ ozs. per coupon	
Sugar	8	8	8	24	21	10

Emergency Cards (R.B.7) entitle holders to Civilian Rations.

Special permits are available for Sugar for Domestic Marmalade making, Bee-keeping and Cookery Classes.

The prices, descriptions, etc., in this SUMMARY are subject to alterations (if any) made by the Ministry of Food since 21st FEBRUARY, 1940.

Notes.—(1) **OTHER PRICE-CONTROLLED FOODS.** Maximum prices are also prescribed for **Meat** (including Pork, edible offal, black puddings, sausages and sausage meat containing 50 per cent. of meat), and for **Liquid Milk.** Also, by arrangement with the Ministry, **Margarine** may not exceed 9d. per lb., while cheapest **Cooking Fat** may not exceed 7d. per lb.

(3) **FARTHINGS.**—In calculating retail prices of commodities marked * any fraction of one farthing is regarded as one farthing.

Do you think, in the light of the fact that he just couldn't take his finger out of the pie, that he retired too early?

No, I don't think he did. I don't think I could possibly suggest he could have retired earlier, because he gave me such a free hand – in fact, he gave me a much freer hand when I was Deputy Chairman than when I became Chairman after he retired. I always said to myself: "He's spent himself in making this thing; now someone else has got it. He thinks he ought still to be consulted".

I think by that time he had lost his judgment. I used to go down and spend weekends with him at Longstock House to discuss with him major matters – the pay sheet, the figures and how the branches were working out – but in things like the recruitment of more high-powered chaps, he couldn't bear not to have his advice taken and I would be accused of ruining everything. There weren't many things on which we differed but I think it built up in his mind as a sort of festering sore.

As you know, he started a campaign to get the Central Council to say he should have a quarter of *The Gazette* and that certain things couldn't be done without his agreement. Of course, it wasn't on at all and the Council understood the need to have only one Chairman and they'd got to make do with the one they'd got.

It really was a very difficult time for me trying to stop the Partnership at large, through its communication media, from being more beastly to him than they wanted to be. I kept having to remind them that what they'd got was because of what the Founder had done for them. It was a very unpleasant period and I must confess I didn't quite know how to deal with it. But I think on the whole we got through it reasonably well.

Did he come through it?

I don't think he did. He got through it in the sense that in his later years he used to talk more in sorrow than in anger, whereas in the earlier years it was definitely anger, intense anger. However, that was the first couple of years or so after he retired. When the Council turned down every approach he made to try and get a share of the power, he resigned himself to the inevitable. We still met, and he regarded me almost as a son. I felt very much attached to him.

In the last years of his life our relationship was, I think, one of mutual respect and affection, except that he was sorry that

I was such a pigheaded devil who couldn't see the light when it was laid before him.

What do you feel about him now?

If I were writing as an historian, I should class him as a maverick who was much ahead of his time. To my mind he latched onto something that could be important and that was wanted, but somehow or other he didn't sell it to other people although he made it work in his own organisation. What the moral of that is I don't really know. Certainly the Partnership has gone on long enough to dispose of the argument that it worked only so long as he was there. I think if I have any claim whatever, it is that I consolidated the advances he made, smoothed away some of the raw edges of his rather dictatorial tendencies, and kept everybody in the picture.

But perhaps it's too early to make a judgment. I think it's possible that the basic idea of partnership may emerge to play a much more important part in striking a proper balance between trades unions, representatives of the workers and so forth, and the managements and employers and owners.

I would think that when the history of the 20th century is written, at lowest – and I use the term advisedly – Spedan will be thought of as a 20th century Robert Owen. I think he will always be recognised as at least as important in the 20th century as Robert Owen was in the 19th, and no one would dream of writing 19th century industrial history without including a chapter on Owen.

Sir Bernard and Lady Miller outside their Leckford home in 1984. Lady Miller joined the Partnership in 1927–the same year as Sir Bernard–and worked in Peter Jones before becoming a sportswear buyer. They were married in 1931. Later she worked in the Intelligence department and during the war was a local merchandise adviser in branches near their home in Cookham. Lady Miller took an active part in organising leisure for Partners as Chairman of the Committee for Amenities

F T Jones

Terry Jones is a naturalist of high repute, an expert ornithologist who achieved notable success in breeding rare waterfowl at Leckford. Joining the Partnership in 1938 he spent a lifetime, interrupted by war service in the Navy, close to Spedan Lewis as the curator of his much-loved aviaries. He retired in 1971 and now lives near Crediton in Devon in a small cottage with a commanding view of beautiful countryside. The local community now benefits from his expertise as a judge at local shows.

As a naturalist, what was Spedan Lewis's speciality?

Mr Lewis's particular interest was in wild flowers and you could rarely fault him. He loved what I call the lesser chickweeds – all those things that no one knows – or the dandelion family, of which there are thousands.

I always remember one plant I learnt. We were making Longstock gardens, and went over to Hillier's nursery to buy some lilacs. It was before the modern herbicides and so there were lots of weeds. Mr Hillier was saying: "Well, Mr Lewis, would you like this lilac or would you like that one?" and all the time Mr Lewis was looking at the weeds. Suddenly he said: "Terry, do you realise that's Claytonia?" It had been introduced from the Middle East because in those days people imported grain that wasn't sterilised and it got sown.

After he'd had his first coronary he disliked being left alone. Mrs Lewis, Phyl Kay, Muriel Elliott and Kate Bonnet all boxed and coxed and I would go over some afternoons to give them a break. I always tried to take him a plant. There's a very rare wild sage in this country, a beautiful blue thing, and I had brought some seed back from France, where it is quite common, and was growing it at the Abbas. Mr Lewis sat with his back to the door at Longstock House, and Phyl took me along, opened the door and said "Terry's here". He said, faintly, "Come in, Terry," and when I got round in front of him I said "Have you ever seen this plant, sir?"

"*Where* did you get that?"

He had in fact found it himself. It was very rare in the Plymouth area, but he had been botanising there and had found it. He was telling me all about the expeditions in search of it when Phyl came in with some papers. Her eyebrows shot up and she backed out of the room. When I was leaving she said: "What on earth did you say to make him so cheerful?" I said: "I showed him a flower".

It is sometimes suggested that he was really just a gifted amateur. How good was he as a botanist?

His interest was aesthetic. He enjoyed the beauty, or the curiosity, or the sound, or whatever it was, but his interest wasn't scientific.

Mine's the same. I reckon to know every British bird I'm liable to hear without seeing it, and identify it the moment there's a strange note. For instance, a parakeet flew over here

Part of JSL's collection of insects, all of which he set himself

the other day and of course I was instantly riveted. I knew what it was because it's a parakeet that has become naturalised in England, but it was the first time I'd heard one here.

Mr Lewis's interest was like that. It was purely aesthetic. And his knowledge of individual plants, and of course his bugs and beetles, was phenomenal.

Was his knowledge of flowers extensive?

Of British wild flowers, yes. You would be very clever if you found one he couldn't name. But I think he got more fun out of his bug and beetle collecting then anything else, because in all the other things he paid someone to do it for him – Pat Macarthy, me, or whoever. But with the bugs and beetles he did all the setting himself in the evenings. When he was setting the micromoths, which are moths about the size of greenfly, he had a little microscope, with the wretched creature underneath it, and he would tease its wings out with two cat's whiskers. He spent hours every evening doing it. He set practically the whole collection at Longstock House.

How did you first meet?

I knew of him before I knew of the Partnership because I've bred birds since I was a child. He had a big collection of pheasants and waterfowl which was written up in the *Avicultural Magazine*, mostly by Miss Chawner who wrote on breeding and keeping birds as well as looking after Mr Lewis's. This was about the early thirties, when I was living in Cheshire.

I was taken to a Zoo Council meeting by Miss Knobel, who was secretary of the Avicultural Society. It was she who had found Miss Chawner for Mr Lewis. The Zoo Council meeting room in those days – I believe it's the library now – was a beautiful room with tiered seating and a stage. I said to Miss Knobel: "Who's that man sitting on the right of the stage? I think he's the handsomest man I've ever seen." She said: "Oh, that's Spedan Lewis".

After that initial encounter there was no more connection for some time. Then Miss Chawner wanted to retire and at the same time a Belgian friend of Mr Lewis's, Dr Derscheid, offered me the job of running his collection in Belgium. I very much wanted to take it but Miss Knobel said "Don't. Something better will come along." Whether Mr Lewis had said something to her by then, I don't know.

One of the farm machines
introduced at Leckford in the
early 1930s

About a year later Mr Lewis evidently asked Miss Knobel
if she knew anyone who might be interested in running his collection and she said: "There's a young chap called Terry Jones".
So I was sent down on approval.

What was the interview like?

Well of course, I had no conception of the sort of attitude the
Partners had towards him. There he was, a rich man old enough
to be my father, but that was all. I had no fear of him. We
never had on the estate – the local people didn't either.

I remember being absolutely astounded once when I was in
Peter Jones and had just come out of the restaurant opposite
the lifts. A young assistant shot out of the lift and said "Chairman's in the building!" That would never have happened at
Leckford. They were respectful to him as the boss, but they
were far, far more intimate. The local people always referred
to him as "Father", as we all did. I was always astounded at
this terror of him, because it didn't exist among any of the farm
people.

What did he ask you to do?

He had this big collection of waterfowl and other birds, and he wanted someone to run it.

Before the war there were a lot of large collections which were purely a rich man's hobby. We kept flamingoes and all kinds of birds that you can't make any money out of. We had the gibbons there. In fact, we bred the first gibbon in England. Then, after the war, Mr Lewis asked me if I thought I could make the collection pay for itself. I said that provided I could sling out various birds that didn't breed but were very nice to look at, yes, I could. After that I had a completely free hand.

It was a strange contrast, wasn't it, between the dynamic man of business and the man who sat and gazed at bugs and beetles?

No, I don't think so, because he worked to the point of exhaustion. He just couldn't stop working – Phyl and Muriel would be taking dictation at eleven at night. When he'd totally exhausted himself, he'd have two or three days to recharge, when he didn't do any work at all. That was when we botanised or bird-watched.

How do you rate the work he did on the estate at Longstock?

I suppose he put the farming side on more of a business footing. He didn't have any agricultural expertise himself but he had Mr Hollis and one or two other advisers. We had the first corn dryer in the country at Leckford. It was a funny old thing, very high and driven, I think, by coal. He introduced modern machinery and he planted those great big apple orchards, so although he never claimed to be an agricultural expert, his was the imagination and, of course, the finance.

Did he commit to writing anything that was scientifically worth while?

I shouldn't have thought so. I don't think he wrote much about natural history at all. As I say, his interest was purely aesthetic.

You went with him to South Africa on holiday trips in winter for his health. Did he enjoy the boat?

No. He was a recluse. He didn't like meeting people and the first year we went he ate entirely in his suite. I would bag a lot of chairs up on the top boatdeck and there we stayed all morning until it was time for lunch, when Mr and Mrs Lewis

The bird farm, fish hatchery and eel traps at Leckford

would retire to their suite. When I said to Muriel: "We've time for a quick drink," Mr Lewis said: "But Terry, there's everything in my state room. I've told you to help yourself." What he didn't realise was that Muriel and I liked meeting the other people on board. Mr Lewis would know everything about his steward's family and lifestyle but he wouldn't be on "good morning" terms with anyone on the boat.

Did he make friends on the estate?

In those days before the war people called and left cards, and the Lewises were, of course, up in London all week. When they came down at weekends they brought buyers or other people down with them, and the Partnership went on at Leckford Abbas. So they had a card printed which they sent round to anyone who had come to call, saying they appreciated them calling but hoped they would understand that they preferred to make their friends in the Partnership. No one ever again took any notice of them and the Lewises couldn't have cared less. I don't ever remember them having the neighbours in.

He knew everyone on the estate by name and would chat quite happily. And, of course, people like Mr Miller, as he then was, and Donald Radermacher and others, came down every weekend, so they were never without company.

Did you ever fall out with him yourself? Did he listen to your advice?

I don't think he ever listened to my advice, but we never fell out.

But going to South Africa with him meant you must have been closer to him than most people.

Probably. The nearest I can say is that it was a father-son relationship. I was young enough to be his son and I had all his outside interests, which neither of his surviving children had. When we went round the estate he was always poking into hedgerows to look for a lesser chickweed or something, and I was interested in that sort of thing too.

When we were in South Africa, he would call me and we would march up and down the lawn. He was planning what he was going to dictate and he would tell me all about what he was doing and who was doing what. It went in one ear and out the other, because it was nothing to do with me. He wasn't really telling me anything, but was talking aloud till he'd got it all straight. Then he'd yell for his secretary and back he'd go to the dictation.

This energy is astonishing – he seemed to work from early morning till late at night.

He never stopped. And under real pressure he dictated in the bath. Phyl sat outside with the door ajar.

Did he have an extensive knowledge of animals?

No. He wasn't really very good with animals. He was frightened of dogs. I acquired a dog in Egypt. She was curious in that she didn't like being touched, so if you bent down to pat her and didn't look, you always missed. When we were making the Longstock gardens I went over every day to help Mr Lewis. When I was in the house Dinah chased rabbits in the garden, and if it was time to go and she wasn't there, I would walk back to Leckford and she followed when she realised I'd gone.

On one particular occasion I had left and, as Dinah did constantly, she'd nicked the tip of her ear rushing through brambles, and it was bleeding. She appeared at the window when Mr Lewis was walking up and down dictating. When he saw her dripping with blood he told Phyl to bring her in. Dinah was put on cushions by the fire and given brandy–lots of it.

Phyl rang me up and said: "Dinah's been seriously hurt. She's torn her ear". I said "Phyl, she does that every day. Fling her out; she'll come back". "It's an order from Mr Lewis," said Phyl. "You've got to come over and get her."

I hadn't a car in those days, so back I had to walk, all the way to Longstock House. There was Dinah, a bit bleary-eyed, lying by the fire, propped up with cushions. I thanked Mr Lewis, picked the dog up and when I was outside, flung her to the floor, only to find she couldn't stand. I had to carry her the whole way back to the Abbas because she was dead drunk.

He kept some quite dangerous animals, didn't he?

When he was a boy he kept various forms of poisonous snakes. Another lovely story – we were in South Africa and everyone had seen a snake except Mr Lewis. Whenever we were out with him we never seemed to see one. One day we had been round the Rondervlei bird sanctuary with the curator and his wife, whose house was in the grounds. It was very sandy and

The Water Gardens, Longstock

Mr Lewis and I had got sand in our shoes. We stopped to shake out the sand and Mrs Lewis, Phyl and Lynnet went on to make a cup of tea. When they got to the lawn, they saw a cobra. Phyl came back to tell Mr Lewis there was a cobra on the lawn. Not knowing animal reactions, they'd left Lynnet watching the snake, with her eyes on the end of stalks. The snake didn't care for being watched, so it slithered away. By the time we arrived it had gone, and Mr Lewis said in exasperation: "But Lynnet, why didn't you *stop* it?"

Tell me about Glyndebourne.

I am probably the least musical of people, but I *love* colour and form, so I thoroughly enjoyed Glyndebourne. In 1939 I was to be taken to see *The Marriage of Figaro*. He had a very good radiogram in the drawing room of the Abbas, and we were all given scores and told to listen to *The Marriage of Figaro*. I can't read a note of music, so when the Lewises turned over the page, I turned over mine.

When we arrived at Glyndebourne, blow me down, we're handed out the scores again. I said: "No, not tonight, sir, I'm going to watch" and he said, "Terry, you're going to listen". I said: "No, sir, I'm going to watch". For years afterwards he gave away tickets and every year he said to me: "You're not musical, are you, Terry?" and I had to say no. Right at the end of his life he said to me: "You don't care for Glyndebourne, do you?" and I replied: "I simply *adore* it".

I suppose the Longstock water gardens are, in a way, his greatest monument as a naturalist?

Thinking of him I remember we were making the big herbaceous border at Longstock which was 100 yards long and about 16 to 20 feet wide, and everything was done on paper first. He loved putting pink and yellow together – I always achieved it somewhere in the garden, but personally I detest it. There were bright pink phlox and yellow helenium coming together in his scheme. I said: "We can't have that strong pink and yellow together". Muriel didn't care for it, nor did the head gardener. He looked at me with a smile and said: "You must remember that good taste is always a minority taste".

We had great fun making the water gardens. It wasn't all planned on paper. Mr Lewis had the bright idea of tying a rag to the top of garden canes – Muriel and I each had a golf bag

full of them. Muriel would stand on one side of the pond or
stream we were going to create and I on the other. "Terry, a
little further to your left; Muriel forward a bit . . ." and so on
until we had made our stream. Then we'd go to the other end
to look at it, decide this doesn't look right, or that doesn't look
right, and alter it all. That's how it was made.

If you walk from Longstock House by the middle path, just
before you get to the bottom where the big cherries are, there's
a big group of little cherry trees. When Mr Lewis retired, Jill
gave him two groups of trees. There were 70 crabs that go down
the road from more or less the entrance to Longstock House
to the water garden. That was his age. The other is a group
of 50 which was the years he'd been in the Partnership.

Well, you mustn't have a straight line. We put the canes in
for the 50 trees, then walked round. I defy you not to get a
straight line somewhere, from some angle. It took us about two
days to place them, merely altering canes, because he would
not have a line from any angle you might want to look at them.

Are you glad you didn't go to Belgium?

Yes, of course I am. He altered my life utterly. There were so
many new avenues. He could never make me musical but I
wouldn't have understood a great many things I understand
now. If you work closely with someone, you're bound to be
influenced by them.

57

P May

Paul May was one of a select group of brilliant young men with whom Spedan Lewis surrounded himself. On leaving Westminster School, he achieved a First in Classics at Christ Church, Oxford, and, after a slightly stormy start with the Founder, pursued a career in the Partnership which took him to the senior jobs in buying, finance and research. He was Deputy Chairman to Sir Bernard Miller from 1955 until his retirement in 1970.

Like Sir Bernard, he took on public duties, being awarded the CBE in 1970. As the interview reveals, he was close to Spedan Lewis and enjoyed, usually, the robust exchange of ideas that helped to shape the Partnership. He now lives in a lovely old house near Alnwick in Northumberland, with his second wife Frances (his first wife died in the early 1960s). His son, Stephen, is the Partnership's Director of Personnel.

I first met Spedan in, I think, September 1927. I'd just finished my first year at Oxford and my father's finances went wrong. I had a scholarship but it didn't in fact pay anything like the full cost, and as I wanted to be completely independent I went to see the headmaster of Westminster for advice. Spedan was also an Old Westminster. He'd been talking to the headmaster about wanting promising learners, so I was sent along to see Spedan. He took me on, and I started as a learner in the "Long Silk Shop" in the old Oxford Street John Lewis.

My tutor at Oxford was an Old Westminster and Mike Watkins, who had been a master at Westminster in my time, had just joined Spedan. The three of them got together, with the result that they discovered a thing called the Fund for Indigent Old Westminsters, from which my scholarship was increased. I was reluctant to go back on that alone, because I wanted to be no more cost to my parents in the holidays or anything like that. So Spedan said: "All right, you're going back to Oxford – as my deputy – because I wasn't allowed to go as I was advised my father's health was such that if I wanted to join him I must do it at once. I will lend you £100 a year (a lot of money in those days) for the next three years, to enable you to go back. All I need is a life assurance, no interest."

So I went back to Oxford. He also said: "In order that you may go back with a quiet mind, I will write you a letter offering you a job when you come down at such and such a rate of pay", which he did. That was a very kind and generous thing to do, and I think too few people know that side of his character.

What was your first impression of him?

I thought he was like a rather awesome headmaster, and in those days, of course, headmasters were people you were very frightened of.

Why did you want to work for him?

I don't think that is the right question to ask anybody who was looking for a job between 1927 and 1935. One wanted a job, and one didn't interview one's prospective employers in those days; they interviewed you. So I was very happy to take the job, and then I went back to Oxford for three years and at the end of my time I decided *not* to take Spedan's offer of a job. I took a post with the United Africa Company and went to the Gold Coast.

It's very difficult to look back. I'm not sure I knew what my reasons were at the time, but I would think it was probably a combination of three things: an instinctive feeling that some corrective was needed after four years of rather abstract mind-training at Oxford; a niggle as to whether I should be wise to work for Spedan – would it be rather a sink or swim prospect?– and a wish to pay off my debts as soon as possible so that I could get married.

I then saw another side of Spedan. I wrote to him to tell him I was going to West Africa and I didn't mention anything about my debt because it didn't seem to me to fit in with that letter. And I got a furious answer from him, saying: "What about my £300?" So I borrowed the money elsewhere and he got it back straight away.

From West Africa I wrote him a long letter and after 12 months I got a reply and he asked me to stay with him on my return. I wanted to get married; I knew West Africa was no good for my future wife; in 1932 employment was very difficult; Spedan invited me in again on a three-year contract of £500, £600, £700 a year, which in those days was a *very* good rate of pay, and I was able to get married the following year. I think it highly unlikely I would have found anything like that anywhere else at that time – 1932 this was.

What kind of people did he attract and why?

I think he attracted the sort of people who would have made high grade civil servants or academics, if they hadn't wanted to have a more concrete career. He attracted people of high standards of behaviour, whom you could completely trust as colleagues and who were attracted by a career which, with its ideal of partnership in industry, offered an interest beyond merely making a living. Max Baker at his retirement party said: "We are lucky that there is a Partnership and that we are in it" and at mine I said the same. Also, Spedan paid high and offered very good prospects to those who proved successful Partners.

As you grew to know him better, how did your impressions of him develop or change?

I didn't see much of Spedan before the war. I was still greatly in awe of him and doubtful that I should survive long term, but I was by then hooked on the Partnership's trading principles and beginning to understand his ideas of Partnership.

I can think of only two meetings in those years, about the mid-thirties, I suppose. Spedan asked me to have lunch with him and I thought it was extremely ominous that he spent the whole of lunch explaining to me that he thought he wouldn't engage any more Firsts because they were all burnt out. I thought that was a prelude to receiving a letter.

The second incident again shows Spedan's great sense of decency which he often obscured. He'd appointed himself Director of Selling at about the time we took over the D H Evans building. He had a meeting of piece goods buyers – I was at that time buying the fancy end of the silks – at which he explained how he was going to lay everything out. There was one very awkward space and he said what he was going to put in it. He said: "That must be the best idea" and he went down the assembled row of piece goods buyers, about six or seven of us I suppose, and said "Do you agree? Do you agree?" All the others said "Yes" and like a silly clot I said "No", because I was quite sure it was the wrong place for that merchandise. Well, this was all done again, and again I said no, and he dictated a paragraph saying: "All the others agree but Mr May, obviously for the interests of his own department, is differing". So I said: "Do you think, sir, that is quite fair? This is miles away from my department and it can have no conceivable effect on it." "Oh. Strike the paragraph out."

After the meeting he took the trouble to walk downstairs with me and be very friendly and talk commiseratingly about the state of trade. He wasn't a chap who objected to being answered like that.

Then there was the war. At the end of the war I wondered whether I should be wise to return to the Partnership or not. I've always suspected that my personal file has more than one draft letter of dismissal on it, but of course I don't *know*. In the end, I was really brought back by the standards of the Partnership and of the people I worked with, and by interest and pride in the job that the Partnership was doing, which is only another way of saying: because Spedan was in charge and had shaped it so. So one can say, in that sense, Spedan brought me back.

A few years after the war I joined the central management and did work closely then with Spedan. I came to believe that he had a real genius, great imagination, and that his approach to both people and business had a strong element of the naturalist experimenter. Try anything that looks promising, scrap it if it doesn't work, and now and then pull the plants up to see how the roots are growing. This showed itself not only in his wide-ranging engagement of people but also in his taking over or starting of businesses – factories, small shops, varied department stores, food trade, shops in South Africa and so forth. This experimental period went on pretty well until his retirement in 1955, and it was only in the early fifties that we began to develop firm policies for department stores, for the food trade and for manufacturing, to complement Spedan's firm policies on Partnership and on merchandising.

His ideas on how business should be organised were very far ahead of his time and, unfortunately, still remain so.

I came to have very great respect and admiration for him, and also considerable affection.

Management techniques: he advised, criticised in no uncertain terms and drove people in person or by memorandum. He had no time for dilatory or slipshod methods and he expected all members of the central management to know everything that happened in their own fields anywhere in the Partnership. At the same time, he was sensitive to people's reactions and if he wanted to keep you in the Partnership he knew when it was time to ease the pressure.

I remember on a number of occasions when I was going to Longstock for the day, saying to my wife: "I've had about all I can take from Spedan, so don't be surprised if I'm not in the Partnership this evening". And on those days he was always full of sweet reason. He was very clever at that sort of thing.

What were the qualities that made him succeed?

Well, I think in his own way he was a genius. He was singleminded in devoting every minute to forming the Partnership and giving it a satisfactory commercial base. His imaginative concept of Partnership, his very keen quick brain, his clear understanding of merchandise techniques, his determination, his ability to attract and retain the respect and affection of good brains with his standards I think made failure an impossibility – unless his need to experiment had led to too wide a dispersion of trading and too little cohesion. He retired before this could happen, but I believe that for this reason the Partnership only began to work as he intended it should work, both as a social and as a trading organisation, after he had retired.

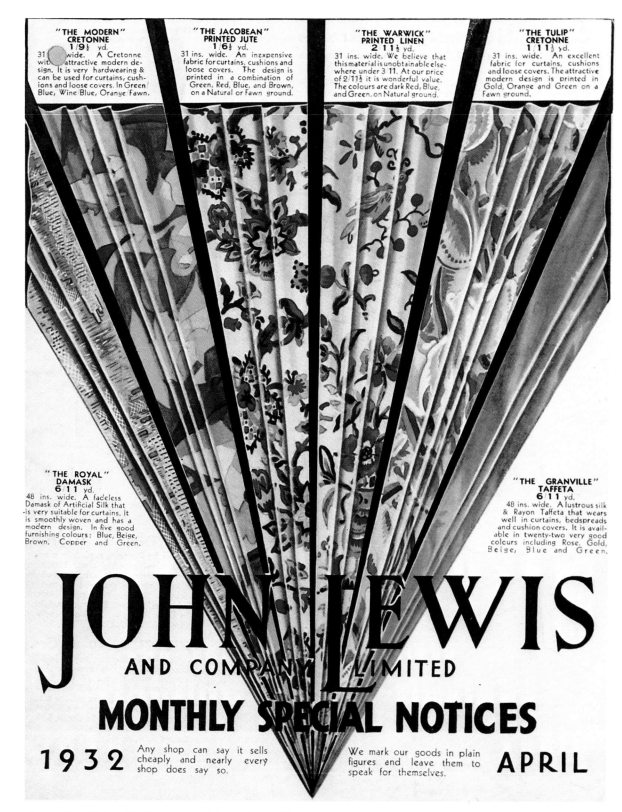

"THE MODERN" CRETONNE
1/9½ yd.
31 ins. wide. A Cretonne with an attractive modern design. It is very hardwearing & can be used for curtains, cushions and loose covers. In Green, Blue, Wine Blue, Orange, Fawn.

"THE JACOBEAN" PRINTED JUTE
1/6½ yd.
31 ins. wide. An inexpensive fabric for curtains, cushions and loose covers. The design is printed in a combination of Green, Red, Blue, and Brown, on a Natural or Fawn ground.

"THE WARWICK" PRINTED LINEN
2 11½ yd.
31 ins. wide. We believe that this material is unobtainable elsewhere under 3 11. At our price of 2/11½ it is wonderful value. The colours are dark Red, Blue, and Green, on Natural ground.

"THE TULIP" CRETONNE
1/11½ yd.
31 ins. wide. An excellent fabric for curtains, cushions and loose covers. The attractive modern design is printed in Gold, Orange and Green on a Fawn ground.

"THE ROYAL" DAMASK
6/11 yd.
48 ins. wide. A fadeless Damask of Artificial Silk that is very suitable for curtains. It is smoothly woven and has a modern design. In five good furnishing colours: Blue, Beige, Brown, Copper and Green.

"THE GRANVILLE" TAFFETA
6/11 yd.
48 ins. wide. A lustrous silk & Rayon Taffeta that wears well in curtains, bedspreads and cushion covers. It is available in twenty-two very good colours including Rose, Gold, Beige, Blue and Green.

JOHN LEWIS
AND COMPANY LIMITED
MONTHLY SPECIAL NOTICES

1932

Any shop can say it sells cheaply and nearly every shop does say so.

We mark our goods in plain figures and leave them to speak for themselves.

APRIL

Above: Furnishing fabrics, 1932, and (opposite) a silk sampler showing 312 different shades available in one quality of silk alone from the silk department in the 1930s

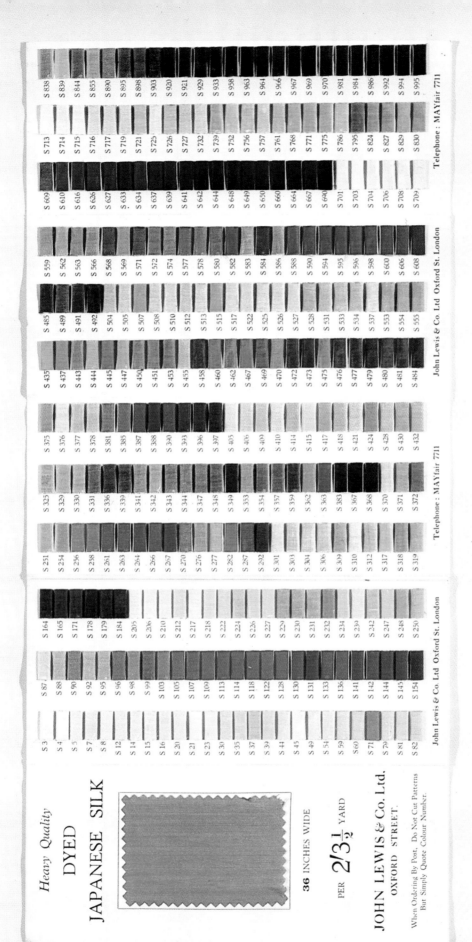

Heavy Quality

DYED

JAPANESE SILK

36 INCHES WIDE

PER **2/3½** YARD

JOHN LEWIS & Co. Ltd.

OXFORD STREET.

When Ordering By Post, Do Not Cut Patterns But Simply Quote Colour Number.

John Lewis & Co. Ltd Oxford St. London

Telephone: MAYfair 7711

John Lewis & Co. Ltd Oxford St. London

Telephone: MAYfair 7711

What were his defects?

No genius is a genius in everything, and Spedan was no exception. Some points of criticism have emerged and others will appear later. I must stress here three points I think to be important. As an experimenter he was curiously blind at times to what he was doing to individuals. He could be incredibly kind and he did a vast amount to help individuals, financially and otherwise, so quietly that none of it was generally known. On the other hand, he was ready to engage widely, sometimes someone already well established in a different career, with optimistic forecasts of the future if all went well, on the general view that a person with the ability that he'd shown elsewhere, and a good mind, might be good for the Partnership. If it didn't work out, then the Partnership must not suffer, and they either had to leave or be content with a post below their expectations on joining. He could be quite arbitrary in this. An experimenter experiments and if it doesn't work cuts his losses and does not repine. And, as I said, he was curiously blind to the effect he had on some individuals.

Secondly – this is a personal opinion which may be quite wrong – I believe he never really applied his mind to, and therefore didn't understand, the difference for central management between running a single shop and a group of widely spread shops. He always appeared to believe that just as he had known everything that happened when he was running Peter Jones, so central management should know everything that happened in the group. He never really fully managed the Partnership once it had become extended.

Thirdly, as he lived on capital, he never applied his mind to, and therefore never understood, personal taxation, or the position of people living on very limited incomes. He had great sympathy with people like that but I don't know that he really understood how near the collar in those days – far more than today – people lived.

The fact that he never understood taxation led him to invent systems such as the so-called remuneration accounts, designed to give promising people a larger income at an earlier stage. This got some Partners in the long run into tax difficulties which took quite a lot of unravelling.

Another mistake of his led to the Partnership adopting a system for cutting wages and salaries by fixed percentages—all approved by the Council and embodied in the rules—if business was bad and profits were falling badly. Fortunately, when the need for applying this system arose, it was applied in a very limited way, and the experience made it quite clear that the whole idea should be forgotten, as it was.

Central management of any experience was left pretty thin on the ground when Spedan retired and I think most of us remaining were quite surprised to be still there. The four years of handover from Spedan to Sunny [Sir Bernard Miller] were much too long and very far from easy. There was one point in those four years when I did jolly nearly leave. I was offered a partnership elsewhere, but when it came to the point I found I just couldn't leave the Partnership and the other chaps. I was too much hooked on the whole thing by then.

What was he looking for in his recruits?

When Spedan went into the retail trade, it was considered a very low class job. A gentleman could *just* be a wholesaler, but certainly not a retailer. I've never forgotten how very much upset my godmother was when she heard I was going into the retail trade. "You *can't* do that," she said. Spedan saw that trained minds could be applied with benefit in retailing as much as in any other activity. He set himself to engage a wide range of abilities not usually found in the trade – the tastes of a McDermott or a Hogg, the highly developed minds of a Watkins or a Miller; some of the top buyers and specialists from elsewhere in the trade, people like Walter Halstead and the piece goods buyers Thomas, Ledbrooke, Hughes and so forth – they were all at the top of their particular walks of life. In short, people who he believed could raise the standard of our retailing aesthetically and organisationally.

Did he recruit many men or women who stood up to him?

That isn't easy to answer because it suggests confrontation and that was not always the best way to get what you wanted. For example, in the early fifties Spedan returned from one of his winter visits to South Africa, having nearly bought a hotel for us but thank goodness not quite, and all lit up with the idea of buying a group of department stores – I think there were five or six of them – in South Africa. He brought back with him their representative to negotiate. I was Financial Adviser at the time and I, and I think all my colleagues, were absolutely dead against this. But if we'd gone into immediate opposition,

we should have had those shops. It took some three weeks of
meetings to make Spedan see what was involved in manpower,
organisation and finance, and gradually his enthusiasm waned.
He reluctantly said no, and sent the representative home
disappointed.

There were the odd occasions for all of us when we had to
say no to Spedan straight away. One didn't do it to him more
often than one absolutely had to. But to be fair to him, I don't
think there was ever in this any risk to our jobs. I don't believe
he would ever have sacked anybody for genuine disagreement
backed by reasonable argument.

Did he ever become a friend of the senior people he recruited?

It depends what you mean by friend. Affection and respect, yes,
but to be friends in the true sense of the word, you have to
be able to talk quite freely together and say always exactly what
is in your mind. I doubt myself whether it would be proper
to describe any of us as his friend in the full sense of the word.
There might have been perhaps three or four exceptions, but
I can't be certain of this. Spedan's whole life, except for his
great interest in natural history, was wrapped up in the Partnership, but I think at times he must have been quite a lonely man.

Jessops' hosiery department
c 1937, showing an early use of
the 'Jonell' brand name

Into what stages would you separate his achievements in retailing?

I think possibly one could separate them into three periods. The
first period: getting Peter Jones on its feet, getting in better
quality people there, and ending up with John Lewis – I suppose
that was about 1927 or 1928. People point to the profits made
at Peter Jones in the years he was bringing it up, and sometimes
are a bit inclined to say: "Well, he didn't do much, look at the
profits". But I think the measure is getting a shop that was going
downhill onto its feet and getting started there the Partnership
systems, then beginning to bring in better people, and so preparing a base for joining up with John Lewis, linking those two
shops together and then going further in expansion.

From then until the early fifties I don't think I would differ-
entiate much. It was a period that I should call experimental
expansion, which began in 1933 with the purchase of Jessops
and the other three out-of-town branches. Also about that time,
central buying, begun to some extent earlier for John Lewis and
Peter Jones, really got going. He was one of the first, certainly
in the department store field, to see that if you are going to
be a group, it is absolute nonsense if you don't have central
buying. You must take advantage of your buying power.

THE GAZETTE

(First issued 16th March, 1918)

OF

THE JOHN LEWIS PARTNERSHIP

begun in 1914 with Peter Jones, Sloane Square, London and now including also John Lewis and Company Limited of Oxford Street, London, Clearings Draycott Avenue, London, Jessop and Son Limited of Nottingham, Lance and Lance Limited of Weston-super-Mare, Knight and Lee of Southsea Tyrrell and Green Limited of Southampton, Crawford Street Garage Limited, Crawford Street, London, John Lewis Properties Limited, John Lewis Building Limited, The Odney Estate Limited, Cookham, Berkshire Waitrose Limited of 21-23 Gloucester Road, S.W.7, 286 Fulham Road S.W.7, 3 The Parade, Ealing, W.5, Castle Hill, Windsor, 158 Ewell Road, Surbiton, 450 Finchley Road, N.W.2, 124 High Road, East Finchley N.2, 14 Victoria Parade, Muswell Hill, N.10, 18 Golders Green Road, N.W.11 7-9 The Highway, Gerrards Cross, and John Lewis Partnership Limited

THE PARTNERSHIP

is intended to secure happiness for its members in any way that it can but chiefly by acquiring the greatest amount of capital for their separate property in the proportion of their separate parts in the collective effort of the team. Within such limitations, as may arise from their general sense of social obligation, the Partnership is to be conducted always wholly and solely for the benefit of its members present and future. Each Partner is to hold his place in the team so long only as its efficiency will not be increased by his standing down but, once in, he is to be given all possible help to keep his footing.

THE GAZETTE

is intended to play in all of the affairs of the Partnership the part that a Free Press plays in all of the affairs of a Nation. Except where this is clearly indicated, views expressed in it must not be taken to be the views of the Management.

The Gazette is intended to maintain closer touch between the different sections and individual members of the Partnership's total team, especially between the Management and all the rest, than can exist without some such means. You can write to it whatever you like and sign your name or not, just as you please.

The postal address is " The Editor, The Gazette, 76, Grosvenor Street, W.1 " (Telephone, Mayfair 7711). For the Partnership's own letter-boxes envelopes can be marked simply The " Gazette."

The Gazette can be supplied to subscribers outside the Partnership. Such subscriptions must be paid in advance. Each issue is twopence post free. Contributions, signed or unsigned, of any kind and from any quarter, are welcome.

Front page of The Gazette, 1938, listing all branches including the Waitrose grocery shops

By Appointment to His Majesty King George V.

WAITROSE STORES
8/9, THE HIGHWAY, GERRARDS CROSS
Telephone Numbers 728 & 729

7 West End Stores under one roof

Departments—FRUIT, FLOWERS AND VEGETABLES, CAKES AND CONFECTIONERY, READY-TO-SERVE FOODS, FISH AND POULTRY, PROVISIONS, GROCERIES, MEAT   ::   *Finest Quality Goods only*

Wine and Spirit Department: 7, The Highway

By special arrangement we ring up customers at a given time each morning for urgent orders

Five Deliveries Daily in Gerrards Cross and The Chalfonts

WAITROSE. LTD.
Head Office : 21/23, GLOUCESTER ROAD, S. KENSINGTON, S.W. 7
Branches in principal London Suburbs, and in Windsor and Surbiton

Waitrose Gerrards Cross in the 1930s

The purchase of Waitrose in 1937; the purchase of Selfridge Provincial Stores in 1940 – were acts of great courage, I think, but they paid off handsomely, because out of our six pre-war shops four were bombed. A number of factories, a hat factory, a belt factory, a chocolate factory, pottery at Odney, any number of factories of all sorts were tried out. Shops of varying sizes were bought. We started three small shops in South Africa. Then there was the episode of wanting to buy the department stores there. Eventually we persuaded him there was no point in being in South Africa with three small shops, and in 1953 I was sent out there to sell them, which wasn't a very popular job because it lost quite a bit of money.

Then came what I would call the period of rationalisation and consolidation, establishing in our own minds firm policies. You have a group of department stores. You've got central buying. What follows from that? We developed the idea of a minimum sized department store and we formed the view, at that time, that one central buying team in the department store trade should not be asked to deal with more than about 20, just possibly up to 24, department stores. From that it followed that each of your shops ought to be as big as the traffic would bear. So that gave us a basis.

As far as the food trade was concerned, we either had to close down those little shops we had – about 30-odd grocery shops doing a turnover of £1.3 million, and no use to us at all – or we had to turn our minds to something much bigger. I think

it was 1951 that we opened the first self-service and went on from that.

This forming of policies led to sales of some of the smaller drapery and furnishing shops and buying bigger ones. We replaced a number with Bainbridge, which we bought in 1952 and got control of in February 1953, and then Heelas. And we had, during the late 1950s and in the 1960s, to add on to our existing department stores rather than go to new ones. John Lewis was rebuilt, and all the other things happened.

And we developed a policy for what we would manufacture ourselves and what we wouldn't, which, broadly speaking, was that we should never manufacture for ourselves if we could get *exactly* what we wanted in every way elsewhere. If we couldn't, then we would have to manufacture for ourselves.

Into what stages would you separate his achievements in establishing the Partnership?

I think I would have said that the policies, principles and most of the machinery of the Partnership remained virtually unchanged since first started at Peter Jones. I would have thought that we only adapted, not changed them, to meet expansion. And time has gradually made this part or that part work better. I would find it very difficult, I think, to separate it into stages. Virtually every form of partnership – policy, principle, machinery – was there at Peter Jones in the early 1920s. That is what was so startling about Spedan.

Can his idea survive?

I see no reason why it shouldn't survive. Only three things, I think, could break the Partnership. Firstly, if there were any really unfriendly legislation passed, which cut across the whole system. Secondly, if the country really went down the drain economically, which at times I begin to wonder whether it won't do. Thirdly, if the Partnership ever allowed itself to become complacent and began, even faintly, to compromise on principle. It is only too easy at times to have something put to you that is just fractionally outside principle. If you accept that, and allow it, you are on the slippery slope. You can defend a straight line, but you can't defend a wavy one.

* * *

No discussion of Spedan is complete without reference to the events after 1955, which I think had a very simple explanation. I can't remember the date, but at one point Spedan entered on what he called his experimental retirement. It seemed pretty clear to me that when he entered this phase, he expected that he would be continually drawn back into the Partnership to settle differences and deal with central management who had got a bit at loggerheads. But it didn't happen. He found nobody went to him, so he came back. When he finally did retire, I'm pretty clear in my own mind that he had the same idea. He expected all the time to be consulted; he expected the management that he'd left behind not to be able to continue without getting him to resolve difficulties. For a very intelligent man it was strange that he seemed to have learned nothing from his experimental retirement.

Not very long after he retired, I was going down to Southampton to Tyrrell and Green and I thought I'd like to see Spedan. I discovered I could drop in to see him on the way back and when I got there we sat down to tea. There was somebody else staying there, and I couldn't understand why Spedan kept on trying to push this chap back to the river to do some fishing. At last he succeeded in doing it, and he turned to me and said: "Paul, now what do you want to see me about?" I said: "Well, Spedan, I just wanted to see you." "Oh", and he completely lost interest.

I think that's at the basis of the whole thing. If he'd approached the thing differently, he could have had a lovely time going around attending branch council dinners and being

honoured and so on. I take my hat off to him for having actually retired – I never thought he would. At the age of 70 he handed the whole thing over, which must have taken a lot of doing. But he kept this idea that, although retired, he would still be constantly needed. He got more and more upset.

In a sense, it isn't awfully difficult to understand. The Partnership was his creation. He'd not only made the Partnership itself but all of us, in a sense, were his creation, and there we were, taking the thing and no longer asking his advice or opinions about his own baby. It's very human, but very stupid, because it cut him off from a great deal that he would have enjoyed.

I remember, some years later, I was down there to see him again; we were sitting in the water gardens having a talk, and he said: "Paul, why are you doing these terrible things to me?" I said: "Spedan, it's very simple. It's your fault. You brought us all up to put the Partnership first, and that's what we're trying to do." But by that time he'd got an *idée fixe* and he was a very sad man. You can understand why it happened. But it was a very nasty end.

I think there's one other point I'd like to make. When I retired from the Partnership and could look back, I was able to say quite genuinely that if I had my time again, in the same circumstances, I should like to spend it doing exactly what I did. That's a very lucky thing to be able to say.

T G M Snagge

Geoffrey Snagge was not a businessman in the ordinary sense but became one of the best-known Partners. He joined from an unusual background of a former Gurkha officer and seaman. Before the war he briefly edited *The Gazette* and, on returning from distinguished naval service, he worked in the Department of Personnel before becoming the Partners' Counsellor. He took a lively part in dramatic productions and was the creator and first Commodore of the Sailing Club, which made him its Admiral on his retirement. After his retirement he lived on the Leckford Estate and wrote a much-valued column in *The Gazette* under the by-line Barleycorn. After the death of his first wife, Norah, in 1961 he married Dame Nancy Salmon, a former Registrar at John Lewis. He died shortly after this interview, in July 1984.

I believe you actually started the Sailing Club. When was that?

In 1951, I think it was. I was staying with Spedan over at Leck-ford and we were chatting after dinner one evening. I happened to mention sailing, because I was keen on it – I had my own boat – and he jumped at the idea of what a good thing it would be for Partners as a whole to sail. In those days sailing was very much a closed shop for the upper middle classes and outside the range of ordinary people.

It was the sort of thing that set him a challenge and you can read his views in *The Gazette* of 13 January 1951, where he announced that we were going to have a sailing club, or at any rate a yacht. He described his reasons for doing it, which were to bring sailing within the range of ordinary people. It was the equivalent, I suppose, of polo today. I wouldn't have put it past the old boy, if he were alive today, to start a stable for polo ponies.

Was he a good seaman himself?

No, poor old chap, he was very bad. The only time I took him out was when I had to bury his wife at sea. We had bad weather but he stuck it very well. I was extremely anxious because, hav-ing made all the arrangements, I didn't want to have to cancel them. It was a pretty rough passage and the skipper of the boat I'd hired wanted to turn back half way, but I wouldn't let him. I felt sorry for him because it was really a luxury yacht and all the furniture came adrift. For somebody like Spedan who had never been to sea in a yacht of that size, it was a pretty hairy experience. I'd been in them during the war and knew what the boat would take, so it didn't worry me. But I was determined to get it over and done with.

Was he very distressed at losing his wife?

Yes, terribly distressed. However, he went out and dropped the ashes overboard and came home. The old boy behaved magnifi-cently on that occasion. He did what he was told, he was kind, he was at his best. I admired him greatly because it took a good deal of courage on his part. Later on I buried him myself from another boat, but that's a different story.

I didn't realise he was buried at sea.

Yes. There's a chart that marks the spot.

I got him interested in the idea of a sailing club and we built a boat, one of the Lion class. I kept him in close touch with the building and that aroused his interest and I encouraged it for all I was worth. I wrote some articles in *The Gazette* about it, with him, with the result that he gave me every possible encouragement.

I had a specific amount to spend – I've forgotten how much but it was quite a lot – and the time came when I was running out of funds. I wanted to put in a lead keel but I had originally budgeted for an iron keel, which was a good deal cheaper but not as good. Spedan was away that summer and, as I had to give the builders an answer, I wrote to him by express letter, explaining the advantages and disadvantages and saying I was very keen to have the lead keel. I got a telegram back – it was, I think, the only telegram anybody ever got from him – which just said "lead keel".

I got everything I wanted, plus a few things that he suggested.

It was interesting that I had to twist quite a few arms to get people to go sailing.

I remember a little salesgirl ringing me up one day. I'd asked them to be ready at 5.30 in Cavendish Square, and she rang to tell me she was all ready but where was the man to carry her bags? I said: "I'm afraid the man is still here but he'll be round in a minute". Which was me, of course. That was how they thought of it. People never thought of it as just going down to the sea; it was regarded as terribly grand and they expected me to arrive in white flannels and a blazer. However, we broke that down all right.

Now it's grown into quite a big thing, which I'm very proud to see.

We used to go ocean racing. We never won a race but we got a couple of seconds and two or three thirds, and that helped in the sailing world. I was tremendously helped by an old friend called Cyril Winler, who was Commodore of the Island Sailing Club on the Isle of Wight. He was extremely interested in the whole idea and said we could use the Island Sailing Club whenever we liked. That was a wonderful gesture. A lot of people in those days thought "Hell's bells, if we get 'shoppies' into the game, that's the end of everything". In fact, I remember one stupid major chap who was rather rude and openly accused me of "spoiling the sport". I happened to be a member of the Royal Yacht Squadron at the time, so I put on my Royal Yacht Squadron hat and answered him back.

79

Sailing Club regattas

The Commodore of the Royal Ocean Sailing Club, whom I knew, was also a great help. In his speech to two or three hundred members at the Royal Ocean Sailing Club dinner at the Café Royal, he said how glad he was to welcome *Ann Speed* from John Lewis and what a good thing it was. That did an enormous amount to help the club get going, since when it's never looked back.

It was a remarkable thing to do on Spedan's part, considering he had no interest in the sea himself.

Yes. The interest for him was that it brought sailing within the range of ordinary Partners. He didn't mind about the rest. He didn't really mind whether we went on ocean races or not – he was quite pleased, but it didn't mean much to him.

You mentioned The Gazette *just now. How did you come to be its editor?*

Well, I was asked down to Leckford one weekend and I'm sure I was going to be given the sack – Jack Webster will confirm that. We were gradually working round, rather tactfully, to the

fact that I wasn't much use to the Partnership when Muriel Elliott, one of his secretaries, came into the room holding a copy of *The Gazette*. It had a new editor at the time. Spedan took one look at this *Gazette* and saw there was a line round the outside of the cover design. Whereupon he flew into a blind rage and sacked the editor. Muriel said: "What about this week's *Gazette* then?" Spedan looked round, saw me and said: "Can you write?" I said: "Oh yes, sir, I can write" – I thought he meant calligraphy. "Well, you must take on *The Gazette*". Just like that. Which I did, knowing nothing whatever about editing.

It wasn't such a severe task in those days, except that it was very tightly observed by Spedan. Every Monday morning he devoted two hours with the editor and went through *The Gazette* comma by comma. We used to go into those interviews and get slated. He would have *The Gazette* in front of him and every page would be spattered with corrections and exclamation marks in green ink. He criticised everything and, after having flattened you completely and leading you to believe it was the worst editing ever seen, he would chuck it aside and say: "Well, not a bad issue".

I remember one particular morning, he turned over the page and his eye lit on a bit of green ink that he'd scribbled on the page; whereupon he banged down both his fists on the table. He always had red ink, green ink and blue ink in a row on his desk, and they all shot out like the Prince of Wales's feathers. Jack Webster had to mop it up with blotting paper. Thank God that broke the spell. After that I was allowed to go.

Did you have any independence at all as editor?

Not really. Of course, Spedan wrote pages for it and it was quite hard work. I had one Mrs Crossley-Williams as secretary, and then I got a little junior. We three got *The Gazette* out every week. Sometimes I spent all night on it. The best I ever did, I think, was 64 pages.

Sixty-four! Was that because of the amount he wrote?

Mostly. And verbatim reports on the Central Council. But he wrote most of it, and heaven help you if you made a mistake. I remember on one occasion after he had slanged me up hill and down dale for a whole morning, I thought "Hell's bells, I'm not fit for any more of this; I've had enough for one day". So I took myself off to Wimbledon – the Partnership used to get tickets in those days. The very first person I met there was old Spedan. I thought "God, here's where I get my cards". He said: "Geoffrey, what on earth are you doing here *now*?" I said "Well, sir, I've got tickets for the afternoon". "Yes, I know, but you've just missed the most wonderful match. Why weren't you here earlier?" I didn't like to say he'd got there in a chauffeur-driven Rolls Royce and I'd had to go by bus. That was typical of him; he'd forgotten all about two hours earlier when he'd called me all sorts of names.

How did he react to anonymous letters?

He approved of them. I didn't, but I think he was right. I couldn't shake him on it. He said that if people had to sign their names they just wouldn't write at all, and that the system was abused only rarely, which was true. Anyway, he wouldn't have it at any price.

He saw that the anonymous letters allowed people to be free, but what happened when they attacked him?

The letter was published.

82

He didn't mind?

Well, he didn't like it very much, but it was published. Doubtful ones like that I used to send to him before publication, but he never stopped one. Occasionally I had to get the legal people onto it because of libel. But it was libel that stopped them being published, not him.

Did he ever stop a letter himself during your time?

No. No matter what they said, he never stopped one. I did, once or twice – not without legal advice though. If I sought legal advice I didn't tell him about it, which was a little on my conscience. I shouldn't have done it but I'd made a rule never to try to fool him.

   He was a difficult chap to fool. I did it once but it was quite innocent. He'd got bored with the layout of *The Gazette* and I had to produce a new design. He didn't like the typeface, so I had to find another one. I searched around and there wasn't anything suitable. He wanted something like *The Times*, so I got a copy and yes, that was what he wanted. Earlier he'd turned down *The Times* print as one of the ones I'd offered him, saying "That's very nearly right, but it's not what I want". That's the only time I ever fooled him.

Did you stand up to him?

Well, as far as I could. You couldn't really stand up to him. You could argue up to a point, but only up to a point – at least, that was my experience. You had to make your mind up whether you were going to do what he said or lose your job, and I always did what he said. People called me a yes-man, but it was no good being a no-man if it meant losing your job – unless, of course, there was some damn good reason, like being asked to do something dishonourable, but there was never any question of that.

Did you enjoy being The Gazette *editor?*

Oh yes, I did. Because I enjoyed working for him, in some peculiar way – why, I don't know, because he was a tremendous slave driver – but it was exhilarating. There were times when I hated his guts, but somehow or other I had a sort of secret admiration for him. I enjoyed the editorship very much; in fact, I enjoyed it much more than any other job I've had in the Partnership.

One of the interesting things about the Partnership was that he attracted such brilliant men, who you would have thought would have left in a rage, but they stayed. What was his secret?

I don't know. I never understood why I survived. I don't understand now, because I was not at all like the others. I was the only fool in the family. I'd got no degree, I had a bird brain, whereas the others all had double firsts.

I literally had nothing. I had no academic record and I always found difficulty in passing exams. Damn it all, before I joined the Partnership I was gutting fish on a trawler for 35 shillings a week. That doesn't exactly train you for the higher flights of business. It's a mystery to me why I survived.

Can I ask you, since you were in this privileged position of seeing him surrounded by these extremely clever men, whether you have any idea how he managed to control them and inspire them and lead them?

Well, everybody, including myself, was a bit frightened of him. One of them – it could have been Baker – said: "Of course, he controls people by fear. They all club together out of mutual

fear". I think that was pretty true. There was a tremendous spirit of camaraderie between us all, and we closed ranks when someone was getting it in the neck. So much so, that if someone was suddenly transferred from one job to another without notice of any sort, it was accepted. Donald Radermacher, who was a very nice chap, came into the restaurant one morning when we were having coffee. He had been slanged in *The Gazette* for something or other and I said to him: "Hello, Donald. You're still here, I see". He said: "Oh, am I? Where's *The Gazette*?"

Were they being held partly by economic circumstances? They could surely have got jobs as captains of industry elsewhere?

A good many of them did, of course. But the caucus was all keen on the Partnership; very few were not. In those days the senior people always mucked in. Michael Watkins, who was a brilliant Cambridge scholar, used to write things for *The Gazette*; Maurice Fitzroy came out of the Navy and played cricket at Odney, having captained Northants. People joined together in social activities.

You see, when I joined in 1930, I knew practically everybody. There were only about 2,000 of us. You certainly knew everyone by sight even if you didn't know them personally. There was a real Partnership spirit and the Partnership really meant something to them. The Partnership spirit touched something in the minds of liberal-minded people. He put into practice what all of us thought was right. Why it hasn't caught on, I don't know, because it certainly caught on in the Partnership.

Why do you think he did it?

Although he was non-political, I think deep down he felt strongly that it was wrong for him to have so much money, and I suppose that triggered it off. Something bit him, because his brother wasn't like that.

One reason that has been suggested is that, as a Greek scholar, he was attracted to the idea of the city state.

He wasn't really a Greek scholar (at least not beyond the age of 18) but he was a member of the Classical Association where, on alternate years, they had a senior businessman and a scholar as guest lecturer. Spedan's turn came up on the business side and he apparently made a brilliant speech on Greek history, so in effect they had a classical chap three years running.

Can you remember the first time you met him?

Yes, I can indeed. He invited me to lunch at the old John Lewis restaurant. I met him because I knew Sir Algernon Peyton, who was then, I think, Director of Personnel. I was looking for a job and Algy said: "You'd better try Spedan". So he fixed up the lunch.

What did he look like?

He was a tall, very good looking, beautifully groomed man. I think that's the main impression I had of him – his immaculate clothes, and his cuffs, hands and hair all beautifully groomed. He said to me: "How would you like to be a draper?" "Very much," I said. I didn't really mean it. What I meant was that I would very much like to have a job. So he said: "All right, go along and see Mr Watkins" and he started talking about £600 a year, which in those days was an absolute fortune. I'd never earned so much. I went to see Michael Watkins, who brought me down to earth with an offer of 35 shillings a week, which I was very glad to accept.

I was sent to Peter Jones where I worked in the basement underneath the pavement with a real old dragon – I've forgotten her name. I had to write out yellow forms – what for, I hadn't the slightest idea – and the rain dripped through the pavement onto these forms and spoilt them, much to the annoyance of the old lady.

I did that for a bit, and then someone said: "You'd better become a draper". So I was put into the fashion department, of all things. I knew nothing about fashion – gutting fish on a trawler wasn't really a very good training for the fashion trade.

There was an old Lady Somebody, who was a real old 'B' and the story goes that her husband ran away with a girl from Peter Jones. As a result, she had it in for everybody at Peter Jones. She came in and made a most terrible nuisance of herself all the time and abused everyone. I was told to deal with her. As I approached her, she backed away, saying: "Don't you come near me, young man, don't come near me". The lift shaft was just behind her and as I took a step forward, down she went. We were on the bottom floor, so she didn't have far to fall, and my name was made. I was told later that I was to be Goodwill Manager of John Lewis and I'm sure it was because I'd dealt with the old lady once and for all.

Can I make you jump forward now to the time when you were invited to be Partners' Counsellor. How did Spedan announce it to you?

He just rang me up and said "How would you like to be Partners' Counsellor?" I said "Very much" and he said "All right". That was all.

The Partners' Counsellor is obviously the ombudsman of the Partnership. Did that change your view of Spedan?

No, not really. I saw a great deal more of what he was doing and how he was dealing with people. We had one or two turn-ups, which I'm glad to say I won – but then I had a very strong case and he listened.

As Partners' Counsellor you must have seen the more humanitarian side of him. Apparently he could be very kind, often by stealth.

Yes. Underneath it all somewhere tucked away was a very very kind man. It didn't show, but I saw it now and again. He could be especially kind to people of no importance. I remember we were playing tennis at Leckford together and during one of the intervals one of the fashion buyers' names cropped up. "She's in hospital," I told him. "In hospital?" said the old man. "Yes, sir, she's been in a week." He stopped the game and stormed into his office, called for a secretary, sat down with me there and dictated: "Owing to the hopeless inefficiency of Geoffrey Snagge I have only just heard that you are in hospital. Of course you must have six weeks in the West Indies to recuperate." Fortunately, she was a very sensible woman and boiled it down to, I think, a fortnight in Brighton. But that was typical of him.

When you look back at him now, if you were describing him to somebody just joining the Partnership, how would you sum him up?

I think I would say that he was an extremely difficult chap to work for. He was very temperamental. He had a terrific personality and boundless mental energy, and you never quite knew where you were with him. He had a lot of very good points and a lot of very bad ones, but the good outweighed the bad, which were mostly on the surface. I think that's all I can say.

M H Lloyd-Davies

Martyn Lloyd-Davies came to the Partnership in 1938, after Oxford, and returned in 1946 having served as second-in-command of the First Battalion, the Royal Welch Fusiliers. He was at various times, and sometimes in combination, General Secretary, Chief Registrar, Director of Personnel, Partners' Counsellor, General Inspector, General Editor and President of the Central Council. He brought much Welsh wisdom, and the shrewdness of a keen chess player, to all his jobs until his retirement in 1984. He now lives in Kensington with his wife Penelope, who was at one time a Partner.

This is the transcript of a talk I gave at a Central Council training session in March 1984:

I first got to know John Spedan Lewis in 1939. He was a keen and very competent chess player and at that time John Lewis had in its new building (as it then was) in Cavendish Square a chess centre; Spedan often used to come along in the evenings, or on Saturday afternoons, and play chess. I met him there on more than one occasion.

He was, I suppose, about 6ft 2in tall, a well built man with a very strong face and extremely piercing eyes which didn't miss much. He was a man of equally strong character and considerable determination.

Spedan was, to my mind, a curious amalgam of his parents. Old John Lewis was a tough, hard-headed man of business who would look at every penny twice before he spent it – he wasted absolutely nothing. Both his sons, particularly Spedan, inherited this sound business sense from their father.

Spedan's mother was, by all accounts, a kindly, gentle person, and it's not without interest that in the dedication of *Fairer Shares* Spedan wrote: "This book is dedicated to my father, whose service to his customers won for the business he created a reputation so good that it seemed well for the John Lewis Partnership that it should bear his name, and to my mother, who was always in favour not only of fairness but of kindness". Spedan inherited both these characteristics in good measure.

He was an extraordinary mixture. I developed a considerable admiration for his qualities and, by the end, considerable affection, though there were times when the affection was rather dimmed, if I may put it like that. He could be ruthless and tough, and he sometimes took actions that made one wonder how anyone could behave in that way. But they were tough business decisions, which he believed to be in the best interests of the business.

At the same time he could be extraordinarily kind and I've known him perform quite secretly many acts of great kindness.

So you get in this character a dichotomy between a tough ruthless man and a person disposed to good work. What one must always remember is that he was determined on one thing and one thing only – to set up what ultimately became the John Lewis Partnership.

His mother's sense of fairness created in him a dislike of the great gap he saw between the owners of capital – his wealthy

JSL with his mother at a sports
day at Grove Farm, c 1913

father and himself and his brother – and the workers in the
business whose wages were pitiful really, and he set out from
an early age to see what he could do to redress the balance,
which he did with a single-mindedness that had to be experienced to be believed. He ate, drank and slept the Partnership
– there is no other way to describe it.

I recall once, when I was General Secretary, staying the night
at Spedan's flat in St John's Court above John Barnes. There
had been a meeting the night before and he suggested it would
be convenient if I stayed. The next morning, at some unearthly
hour, there was a knock on my bedroom door and one of his
secretaries said: "Martyn, if you are up" – which I clearly wasn't
– "Mr Lewis would like to see you". I put on a dressing gown,

went out of the room and, to my surprise, was ushered into the bathroom. There was Spedan, shaving and dictating. He wished me to hear what he was dictating so that there could be no subsequent misunderstanding on my part that he hadn't actually said what he was saying.

He was ever a great writer of memoranda, but because he was essentially an orator the way to understand what Spedan wrote is to read it aloud. The language flows as if it were an orator addressing an audience.

He was what I believe nowadays is called a charismatic figure. You could not be in a room with him without noticing him being there; there was a magnetism about him that had to be felt to be appreciated and it displayed itself through his great belief in what he was doing, his absolute determination to establish the Partnership, and his absolute determination to see that no one, but no one, got in the way of his doing so. And, as we know, he succeeded, although he was modest enough for many years to think of it as an experiment, because he didn't know how it was all going to turn out.

It was because of his determination to establish the Partnership that he was quite ruthless in his dealings with people. If they didn't serve his purpose they were out – either in a job somewhere else in the Partnership or out of the business altogether.

As far as he was concerned, those who weren't for him were agin him, and while he talked at length about industrial democracy, let us have no illusions: democracy stopped at him. If you want a pen picture of an autocrat, that was him.

He had one quality which I have met in only few people. I have attended many board meetings where he was in the chair; a question would be put to him and a discussion would follow. Mr X would say this and Mr Y would say that, and so on, and quite suddenly this man would throw a shaft of light from a quite unexpected angle and open up the whole discussion in a completely different context – lateral thinking, I believe you call it nowadays.

I shall always be grateful to Spedan for one particular reason. He taught me nothing in the way of administration, because he was no administrator, but he did teach me a lesson I had not really grasped before I joined the Partnership.

When I was about 22, I suppose, he taught me to use my eyes, which may seem a strange thing to say. I had had a normal education and knew more or less how to think straight, but I had never known what it was actually to use one's eyes. Spedan had such an extraordinary eye for detail you could bet on it that if you wrote him a paper and you had misspelt something, or misphrased or omitted something, he would pick it up. And that was worth three pages of strong reproof.

Shortly after I rejoined the Partnership after the war I was invited to lunch at Longstock House, where he was then living. He wanted to find out from me how things were going. He was an excellent host, and so was his wife, and after a very good meal he suggested we go for a walk round the grounds. I can remember the date – 9 July 1946 – and during the walk we went down a pathway where there were some coal sheds. He stopped and said "Good afternoon", like the good country squire, to the man delivering the coal, and as we walked on he said: "Martyn, do you know what was wrong there?" I said "No, the man seemed to be doing his job" and he replied: "Ah! But there was no one there counting that he delivered the right number of bags".

He once took me to a hall near Westminster where the big horticultural shows are held. He was very fond of gardening and he pointed out to me in great detail why a couple of the plants were wrongly named.

Spedan was a considerable personality, but not a great man – great men are few and far between. He was a man of considerable vision and I suspect that without him I personally would not have remained in the Partnership, because I was not primarily interested in commerce. When I came back from the war they tried me on the buying side and Mr Baker, then Principal Director of Buying, astutely recognised he had got an incompetent on his hands and offered me to Spedan to start up a little job he wanted doing. It was just as well, as I hated buying, because nothing could talk back to me. From there on I enjoyed my Partnership career enormously and I owe Spedan a considerable debt for that.

It was not easy. You had to stand up to him because if you caved in you were lost. You had to have a mind of your own and a willingness to express it – he had no time for you if you sought the nearest bush and ducked your head behind it, but if you were able to express a point of view and stick to it and felt you had right on your side, he respected you for it. It was an exciting and stimulating life.

Above: The National Chess
Centre at John Lewis Oxford
Street, in the late 1930s, and (left)
JSL playing chess in 1959

C M Jones

After the war Maurice Jones spent his working life on the Leckford and Longstock Estate, of which he was Managing Director for 30 years until his retirement in 1980. His experience was of Spedan Lewis the estate owner. Under his management the estate became a prosperous farming enterprise. He still lives on the estate, and is Chairman of Hampshire County Council. He remains a familiar and cheery countryman around Leckford and the county of Hampshire.

Tell me about the first occasion you met Spedan Lewis.

It was, I think, in September 1946, when I had just been engaged to come to Leckford Estate as the General Manager under the existing Managing Director of the time, Mr Walter Hollis, and we had a conference in Leckford village about the re-building of the village. A good-looking man, with very intense attitudes, piercing eyes and completely unrelaxed, he asked me where I had fought during the war. He had a high-pitched voice which I found rather monotonous, but his manner was generally very friendly.

He is often described as a charismatic man. Did this come across?

Yes. I immediately thought how highly intelligent he was and completely obsessed with his ideas of the John Lewis Partnership.

Was he a lovable man?

No, I don't think he was. Indeed, I knew him, because he lived in Longstock House – that was his home. I lived across the valley at Leckford and I was responsible for the farming and for looking after his gardens and all that aspect of the business. I could never have said he was lovable. He was a complex man and I cannot think he really made anybody feel loved or relaxed in his company.

Then what hold did he have over them?

He must have had a hold over them, I suppose because they were attracted to his ideas; he paid them well; or if they had known of a better hole, they'd have gone to it. Of course, an enormous number of my contemporaries who started in the Partnership during the five or so years after the war didn't stay more than a year or two.

You obviously saw him in the context of running a comparatively large estate. Did you ever stand up to him?

Oh yes. In the early fifties we had a tremendous problem with housing, and I remember receiving a memorandum from him which said that he'd like to move X to Y, A to B, C to D, and uproot people from their homes to suit himself, so that he could get an extra gardener or install his personal servants. I wrote back to him saying why I didn't think this was the right thing, and I can remember quite clearly saying: "It is a thousand pities

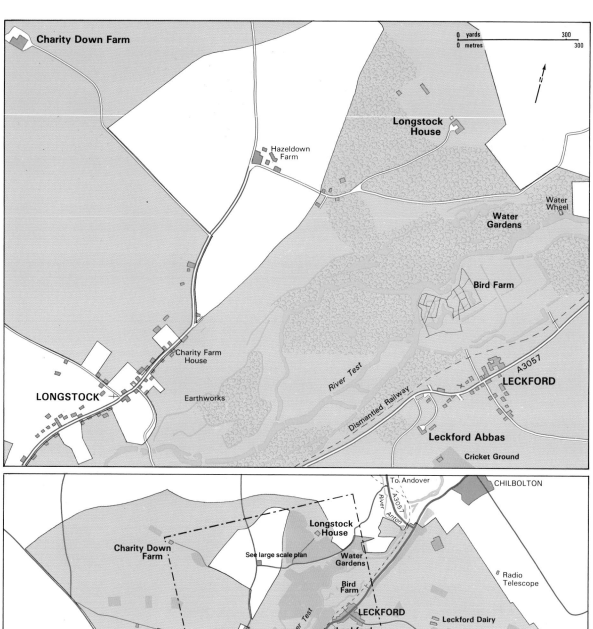

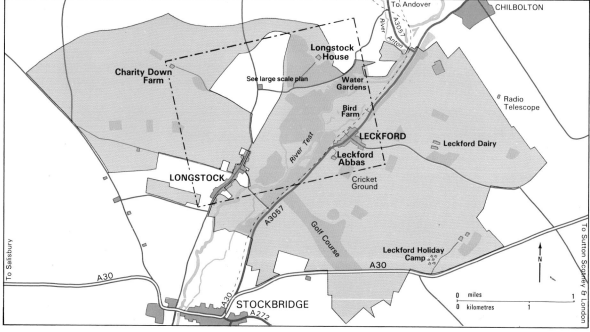

that those who know something about the estate shouldn't have been consulted first before these ideas were put forward".

Above: Longstock House
Opposite: The Leckford Estate

How did he react to that?

I never heard another word and we never moved another person.

How did you rate him as a countryman?

Tremendous knowledge of natural history, tremendous knowledge of plant life, tremendous knowledge of both aquatic birds and pheasants, a considerable naturalist, but he never "gelled" in the countryside. When he first came down here in 1928 and came to live at Leckford Abbas, it was in the days when country people called on newcomers and left their visiting cards. By about 1930 he and Mrs Lewis had not repaid any of the calls and he wrote round to all those who had called and said, in so many words, that he already had an enormous circle of friends in the Partnership and wasn't really able to take part in any further social activities in the county. No wonder, therefore, that when he became an old man, none of the existing county people knew him or cared about him.

Isn't that an example of his utter commitment to his own ideas, even to his own detriment?

Absolutely. It showed his complete obsession with Partnership as a theory and as a practice. But I remember being told that when he went shooting in the early days, if he didn't hit a bird he'd complain that the bird swerved away from him because his chauffeur, Francis, was wearing too broad a checked suit. And I remember Baine, the head water-keeper, telling me that Mr Lewis had stamped on his rod when a trout got off his hook, and he never fished again. So those aspects weren't very laudable in a countryman, but his knowledge of moths, plants and so on was unsurpassed.

I remember once coming up from the water garden with himself, his son Edward, and a secretary. We had been talking about fly-life on the river and he said to Ted something like: "That so-and-so fly always hatches out at such-and-such time of year at such-and-such temperature". Ted said to him: "Oh, I've never heard of that before" and Mr Lewis said "I'm sure I've told you about that". Turning to his secretary he said: "When we get up to the house, look up my files on 'Talks to Children' and see if I haven't already spoken to my children on that subject".

Isn't it remarkable that he obtained for Partners some of the best fishing in England?

Quite remarkable. When I first came, there were very few rods, but slowly and surely we improved the quality of the fishing. Then we were able to keep certain of the rods back for the members of the Partnership and use the income that we got from letting the rods to outsiders to pay for the rods we kept for the Partnership.

What about the gibbons on the estate?

Gibbons evidently have great trouble breeding in captivity, and Spedan, who was chairman or vice-president of the Zoological Society in London, volunteered to see whether they could breed in the Hampshire countryside. He therefore told the estate's previous Managing Director to make an island, because gibbons wouldn't cross water, and to erect a large pole, on the top of which there was to be a nesting hut. From the top of the nesting hut he was to hang pieces of rope, rather like a maypole, so that they could swing round and round. Well, in due course, Mr and Mrs Gibbon did have a child, and daddy gibbon got so excited that he got into one of these ropes, swung himself

round, landed in the Test, got out on the opposite bank and started to walk up towards Longstock, where he met the then owner of Longstock House, a Miss Winnie Beddington.

Miss Beddington, you won't be surprised to hear, had an attack of the vapours upon seeing a gibbon staggering up the river bank at her in the centre of Hampshire. She went home and wrote to Mr Lewis, saying that the sound of the gibbons howling in the Test valley, and seeing them on the river bank, was only what you'd expect from a jumped up draper spoiling the countryside. He wrote back and told her she was a hysterical woman and that it was quite reasonable for a gibbon to be walking up and down the Test bank.

I believe his method of planting bulbs could be idiosyncratic?

Yes. In the mid-fifties we had a head gardener here called Kinch. I was walking through the gardens one day when I found a gardener sitting on an upturned bucket sandpapering horse-chestnuts. He said Mr Kinch had told him to do so. I went to Kinch and said "What on earth is going on here?" Kinch showed me a memorandum he'd had which said that Spedan Lewis had been to the Chelsea Flower Show and had bought 5,000 yellow and 5,000 mauve crocuses. He had also noticed this year that there had been a tremendous fall of horse-chestnuts and Mr Lewis thought that if we put horse-chestnuts into a bag – some white and some the natural chestnut colour – the gardeners could go round the centre park tossing them out, and where the white ones fell we were to plant a yellow and where the dark brown ones fell we were to plant a mauve. Well, said Kinch, "when I tried to put whitewash onto horse-chestnuts, the gleaming skin promptly wiped it off. So I've had to put this chap onto sandpapering them, so that I could get the proper sticking effect of the whitewash."

But the most glorious part was the last paragraph of the memorandum which said: "If, when the gardener has scattered these chestnuts like this, they look unnatural, pick them up and scatter them again".

What about the serious side of his naturalist work? I've been told that his work on breeding some varieties of duck, for example, was significant?

I think that's perfectly true. I would have thought it was more on the tragopan pheasants in the early days. We failed to get

Temminck's tragopan pheasant. JSL bred this rare species successfully in the 1920s.
He was a Fellow of the Zoological Society of London from 1925 and vice-president in 1939. He donated tragopan pheasants on several occasions as well as many other birds and animals. His financial guarantee against loss enabled the society to acquire land in 1926–7 and successfully establish Whipsnade Zoo

in new blood, so we couldn't get the proper hatching rate after the war. I would have said that was even more important than the ducks. Terry Jones was a fine naturalist and it certainly was he who supported Peter Scott in getting the Hawaiian geese over here and in suggesting to Spedan that Leckford should be the first to breed them – which Terry then did.

What in your view were the qualities that made Spedan Lewis a success?

Without a doubt his tenacious application of the Partnership's theories, his tremendous application to make a really good water garden here, and his tremendous application towards ecology in general. But his defects were a lack of understanding of human nature. You cannot imagine a man who would write memoranda to his wife and children as he did. Of course, in consequence, he didn't integrate socially, so his latter years were very sad and very lonely. He was an exceptional man, quite exceptional. Not a lovable man, but a man of great breadth. I would say a jack of all trades but not really a master of any. He was extremely generous. He always entertained us extraordinarily well – excellent wine and food. It was a little bit embarrassing when a secretary had to sit beside him during lunch or dinner to make notes of what you said, either as an interesting facet of life or so that it could be used in evidence against you.

His personal relationships I always thought were pathetic. He didn't inspire me with affection; he inspired me with a certain amount of uncertainty – you never knew which way he was going to jump, and that was very difficult to cope with. I think he had an original mind; he was capable of inspiring the young; but I do not think that, on balance, I could really have great respect for him, except for his philosophy.

Would you agree that a more balanced human being could never have set in train the extraordinary organisation which became the Partnership?

That question ought to be asked time and again. Yes, I think he was brilliant, and he started the organisation, but I also think, seeing it as I did from a close working relationship with him, that if it hadn't been for Sir Bernard building on that foundation, the Partnership would have been in difficult financial straits because of the theory going too far ahead of the practice.

Archibald Thorburn
1912

H E Baker

"Max" Baker was another of the young academics with whom Spedan Lewis surrounded himself. He took a First in mathematics and natural science at Cambridge and had some ten years' experience in industry and retailing before joining the Partnership in 1934. His career, on either side of war service in the RAF, was in buying and selling, his last post being that of Director of Trading, Department Stores, from which he retired in 1967. Since his retirement he has lived on the Leckford Estate and lectured another generation of senior management entrants to the Partnership.

When did you first encounter Spedan Lewis?

I was in a textile business from 1924 onwards. I had known the owner's son at Cambridge, and he had known of my reputation at Cambridge. The son was not particularly bright, and the father persuaded me to join the company, to hold his son's hand. We joined at the same time and were both sent to work in a French textile factory in Lyons for a year. I started at the bottom and within five years was running the business.

Meanwhile, the son had shown no aptitude and had left the business. The father then lost interest and decided to sell up. I wasn't going to be sold with the business, so I got out.

We supplied John Lewis at that time – I supplied the famous Yearsley, the silk buyer – so I knew all about old man John. I knew vaguely about Spedan, but the Partnership wasn't formed until 1929 and I'd left the City and the West End by 1930. By 1934 John Lewis was beginning to make quite a reputation and Spedan was writing in the trade papers about his Partnership scheme.

His general ideas of co-operation and Partnership appealed to me and one weekend, in May 1934, I wrote to him, saying: "I wonder whether a chap with the following record would be of any interest to you". I wrote to him on a Sunday, posted the letter on Monday, and on Wednesday morning had a reply saying: "I am very interested indeed and I would like to see you as soon as you can conveniently manage it".

I was working at Lewis's Ltd in Birmingham at the time. Wednesday was our half day, so I took the train that afternoon and arrived at Cavendish Square at about 3 o'clock. Spedan was rather taken aback but said he would see me in five minutes. I had three-quarters of an hour with him and was engaged then and there. He was busy; I'd sprung my visit on him and, contrary to his usual habit of confirming everything in writing, he said "I'm too busy to write to you. I want you to come as soon as you can; will you please write and confirm the substance of our agreement".

When you walked through the door on that day in 1934, what confronted you?

A very handsome fellow, tall, with chiselled features, immaculately dressed, and an impression of being "on the ball". I told him what I'd done at school and university, and in the

City and so on, and I'd sent him various highly complimentary letters I had received from tutors and dons when I left Cambridge. (It was always assumed I would stay on and become a don.) He asked me about my job as group merchandising manager at Lewis's, and what I actually did all day.

What job did Spedan offer you?

He engaged me to run the West House of John Lewis, which at that time was run by Donald Radermacher, whom he moved to Peter Jones. Spedan gave me three weeks with Donald and then I took over. By reason of the drill that had been established I inevitably came into frequent contact with him. This was in 1934, at the height of the Depression and piece goods were no bet then. West House's success depended above all on its dress piece goods and its soft furnishings. It was a hard struggle and the drill was that every branch – by that time there were six – was expected to put on a minimum of 10 per cent in trade. If they did, no questions were asked; if they didn't, one had to send a report to Spedan, who was not only Chairman but Chief Executive. In fact I was writing to him nearly every week.

That was an education in itself. You had to judge what you said. I only remember getting a critical comeback once, when I referred to the trade on the third floor. His comment was: "It tells me nothing; I don't know what the trade is on the third floor". I apologised and explained that what I should have said was the trade of the departments on the third floor. It was a lesson in being precise.

Looking at your contemporaries of that time, what sort of people was he attracting into the business?

His principle in running the business was that the most important part to look after was the buying side, and he looked after that personally. He engaged the buyers himself and personally reviewed them every six months. Mike Watkins once said he thought that practice was one of the most valuable that Spedan had introduced. Some senior buyers were also company directors of the business and were highly paid – one was paid more than anybody else in the business, except for Spedan himself.

Was he as shrewd on the selling side?

He didn't spend much time on the selling side. Buying was his immediate responsibility and his first priority, and as he couldn't give as much time to everything as was necessary, the selling side – except for the routine reporting if the sales weren't up to the minimum requirement – was not under quite the same spotlight as the buying side. When I joined the Partnership, he hadn't started reviewing the heads of branches. I was the first one. My review, which took the form of an interview in his office, lasted for three days, and the report ran to 56 double pages.

How detailed was his knowledge?

Well, the buying side was a splendid machine when he eventually handed it over. It was unquestionably the best team in the trade, and he'd reviewed them in detail every six months. Because they were specialists, and because his office was on the first floor of the Oxford Street building and he frequently walked through the shop, he had a thorough knowledge of what was going on.

So at this stage you were fairly senior but not part of the inner circle, as it were. What were your impressions of him and how did people at your level feel about him?

Most people were scared of him because of his reputation with those who had run foul of him. He could fly into an almost uncontrollable temper. He'd been known to throw his hat on the floor and jump on it; and to bang on the desk so hard that the inkwell had jumped and overturned. When he really let go, it was frightening. My wife always used to say to me: "Your great advantage in dealing with Spedan is that you're not frightened of him."

Why weren't you frightened of him?

I suppose for two reasons. I regarded myself as having just as good a brain as he had, and I wasn't afraid of losing my job. Other people were, because they'd seen so many odd and indefensible appointments terminated within a relatively short time. After all's said and done, his taking me on, as he did, in three-quarters of an hour was frankly a bit slapdash.

Who were the very influential men, the tightknit group, around Spedan Lewis before the last war?

Well, it changed in the mid-thirties. When I went there in 1934 Michael Watkins was Director of Research, and was genuinely doing research. Sunny Miller was what subsequently became

GRANTA   **4** Gns.
A slim-fitting model made easy to wear in stock-size by the sash tying at the back.
In Genita (a kind of Jersey-de-Soie). Green, Sapphire or Black.
Size 40 ins. (hips).

GORDON   **79/6**
In Jersey-de-Soie with a softly gathered bodice and cut on flowing lines.
In Black/White, Black/Red, Navy/White, Brown/Rust.
Sizes 40, 42 ins. (hips).

MALTA   **6½** Gns.
A sleeveless Dress and Jacket adapted from a model by Patou. In several designs of Blue and White printed Crepe-de-Chine.
Size 40 ins. (hips).

JOHN LEWIS
AND COMPANY LIMITED

1932   **MONTHLY SPECIAL NOTICES**   **JUNE**

These Monthly Special Notices are sent Free on request.

Three Types of "Sailor"

Very becoming because of the slightly sloping lines of the crown and soft brim. A narrow ribbon threaded through the crown ties under the brim at the back. Leghorn: Colours, Natural, Navy, Nigger or Black, with contrasting ribbon.

Sizes 6⅞ and 7   **19/11**

TRIANGLE SCARF   2/11½

A design of spots and stripes in Artificial Silk of good quality. In Green/White, Blue/White, Nigger/Beige, Black/Gold, Black/Green.

KNITTED SCARF   2/9½

Fine Wool in a lace-stitch. In Yellow/Red/Brown, Pale Green/Emerald/Dark Green, Emerald/Royal/Black, Red/White/Blue, Pale Blue/Royal/Navy, Beige/Tan/Nigger.

A subtly different version of the "Boater" Hat. The Straw is pliable and the crown curved on top instead of flat. In Natural, Navy, Nigger or Black, with contrasting Petersham ribbon.

Sizes 6⅞ and 7   **8/11**

An American Sailor's Cap of brightly coloured wool, with Scarf to match. In Emerald/White, Red/White, Royal/White, Navy/White, Nigger/White or Black/White.

The Set   **7/11**

WAISTCOAT SCARF   4/11

This is a new idea. It combines a Waistcoat front with a scarf that can be tied in various ways. In multi-coloured stripes combining Yellow/Flame/Navy, Green/Yellow/Brown, Red/Green, Royal/Yellow, Flame/Yellow/Black.

WAISTCOAT FRONT   3/11

Artificial Satin in Ivory or Beige fastened with pearl buttons.

Also with collar and rever.   **4/11**

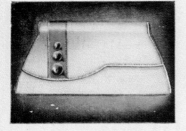

WHITE LINEN POCHETTE   7/6

A new design, with a wide stripe of White, Lemon, Green, Blue or Beige, decorated with three chromium-plated buttons. Silk lined and fitted with a mirror and purse.

BAG AND SCARF   7/6

Made of Artificial Crepe, in Green, Red, Blue or Brown, with large spots of contrasting colours. The Bag is a useful thumb shape and is fitted with a mirror and purse.

WHITE WASHABLE BAG   4/11

(Real Leather)

A really remarkable value. Real Persian Morocco Leather, specially treated so that it can be sponged. Lined with artificial Silk, and fitted with inner division and mirror.

John Lewis catalogues, 1932

Director of Estimates; Seb Earl had been in about two years but hadn't really settled down to a specific job; and a man called Coad Pryor was Chief Merchandise Adviser. Elliot Butler, of the Butler family, was Chief Staff Adviser. Sunny had come in straight from Oxford. He did a long stint as Spedan's PA and then had a bit of a trial run at buying sports gear. He'd gone through the mill. He did a short spell serving in the piece goods deparment but then went to Estimates because it had been decided he wasn't really a trader.

Mike Watkins had a very quick brain and he was the chap whom Spedan in some ways regarded almost as a son – he sharpened his wits with Mike.

After he'd done my review for head of John Lewis, he decided this should be extended to the heads of all branches, as the buyership reviews had been developed. There were now four shops, with ambitions to have more. Spedan was beginning to conclude that the time had come when he couldn't really be both Chairman and Chief Executive. He decided in the middle of 1935 that he was going to "die experimentally". He handed over the Chief Executive job to Mike Watkins and retired to

KINGSTON (The Set). **23/9**
Striped Jumper in Flame, Coral, Billiard Green, Larkspur, Royal, Beige, Nigger or Black. Plain Cardigan. Sizes S.W. and W.

The two people in the little boat are too far away to see distinctly but they are both wearing the new Flannel Beach Shorts. May we send them on approval? They are **15/11**

LYNTON **9/11**
Elastic Knit Swimming Suit with Skirt. In Bottle Green, Wine, Navy or Nigger. Sizes S.W. and W. The Cap (curvilated to look like hair) in White, Yellow, Brown or Black .. **3/11**
A Sunshade in floral Cretonne of good quality, with a straight handle of plain or painted wood. In White, Yellow, Green or Beige. Total length 30 ins. **8/11**

JOHN LEWIS & CO., LTD.   *Page 8*

LYME REGIS **6/11**
Bathing Cape of bright-coloured holiday wear. The wide military lapels fasten up to the throat with gilt buttons. Made of Alpafine. In Lemon, Green, Blue or Beige. Sizes S.S.W., S.W. and W.

ILFRACOMBE **25/9**
An unlined Coat for general holiday wear. The wide military lapels fasten up to the throat with gilt buttons. Made of Alpafine. In Lemon, Green, Blue or Beige. Sizes S.S.W., S.W. and W.

OXFORD STREET, LONDON, W.1.

KINGSLEY **12/11**
Gaily striped knitted woollen Sweater. In Gold-White, Red-White, Sapphire-White, Navy-White, Nigger-White, Black-White or Pink-Black. Sizes S.W. and W.
THE SKIRT **19/11**
FLANNEL TROUSERS **19/11**
In White, Royal, Navy, Nigger or Grey. White Belt, 9/6.

MAYfair 7711.

MIDDLETON **31/9**
This Suède Sports Coat is unlined. In Green, Blue, Beige or Brown. Sizes S.W. and W.
THE SKIRT **19/11**
A gored Skirt of checked woollen material. Excellent for golf or country. In Navy-White, Brown-White or Black-White. Sizes 38, 40, 42 ins. (hips).

PERRANPORTH **4 Gns.**
A "Sports" Coat, well-tailored in good quality Flannel and lined throughout with Crepe. It fastens with Nickel buttons, and the collar and wide belt are smartly stitched. In Navy, Beige or Grey. Sizes S.W. and W. Spotted Foulard Scarf included.

JOHN LEWIS & CO., LTD.   *Page 9*

MEDWAY **25/9**
Coat of crested Corduroy with Nickel buttons. Lined throughout with Artificial Silk. In Blue, Navy, Brown or Black. Sizes S.W. and W.
THE SKIRT **17/11**
Made of Beige or Grey Flannel, or in a fancy woollen material. In Blue, Lido, Navy, Tan, Brown or Black. Sizes 38, 40, 42 ins. (hips).

KEW **12/11**
This dainty woollen Jumper, knitted in a lace-stitch, has a frilled collar in colours to tone or contrast. In Yellow, Orange, Tomato, Lido, or all White. Size W.

OXFORD STREET, LONDON, W.1.

Leckford Abbas. Whereas people like myself had previously reported to Spedan, heads of branches and the buyers would now report to Mike Watkins. Mike would also do the buyership reviews which Spedan had done hitherto. He moved me out of John Lewis and gave me Coad Pryor's job as Chief Merchandise Adviser, which was soon changed to Director of Buying. He gave Coad Pryor Watkins' previous job as Director of Research.

So, in the first instance, the Chief Executive's job was thrown over to Mike Watkins, and what Spedan had regarded as the top priority – the buying side – was turned over to me, but I reported to Mike, not to Spedan. Seb Earl grew into the job of head of the selling side, reporting to Mike Watkins again but responsible for the operation of the branches. More of the estimating and control side – what you might call the financial operations – devolved onto Sunny Miller.

You were all men in your thirties then?

Yes, four of us. Spedan kept an eye on the scheme for 12 months and then said to the four of us: "I want you all to sign an agree-

The handbag department, John Lewis East House, c 1936

ment with the Partnership for the rest of your working lives, until the age of 65. Now that's a tall order, but I've set my mind on it and, because it's a tall order, I want you to form a committee of four and I'll give you the best legal advice you can possibly have" – which was that of Miss Enid Rosser, as she then was, one of the first women to be called to the Bar – "and I want you to draw up your own agreements". Which we did.

Did you decide on your own pay as well?

No, not quite. It didn't matter all that much because the agreements were for life on our side but not on the Partnership's side, which made it somewhat tricky. Seb Earl was married to the daughter of Lord Maugham, who was then Lord Chancellor, and Seb submitted the draft of this extraordinary agreement to him and asked for his comments. Lord Maugham said he reckoned it would hold water in a court of law, but he made one suggestion, which was adopted. Before I tell you what it was, I must remind you that this was 1936, when the worldwide slump was still hitting hard, the biggest problem being deflation. It was extremely difficult to increase your trade because prices were dropping. Lord Maugham's suggestion was that the agreement should provide for index linking against the possibility of inflation. So it was indexed on the basis of prices of 1914.

Did you keep that contract for the rest of your Partnership life?

I've still got it. It's a rare document – there were only four of them.

How did Spedan Lewis relate to you all?

He let us get on with it. Seb and I were reporting to Mike Watkins, with whom he was very close, and of course he had a very good understanding with Sunny Miller, who had worked as his personal assistant for many years.

How did your relationship with Spedan develop after that?

It didn't really. The relationship developed with Mike Watkins. I used to run into Spedan on the relatively rare occasions when he came up to town to see Mike over something or other and I happened to be there.

Tell me about the feeling then among the four of you, who were effectively the men at the core of the Partnership. You weren't relating to him directly but he was still the boss.

No, he stepped out of it for three years. He wanted to see what would happen if he faded out of any active part of the business.

What happened at the end of the three years?

The war broke out and he was happy to leave everything to Mike. He didn't come up to town any more after that.

Looking back, how do you assess the Founder?

Spedan was a very complex character. He always said that everybody is what the Italians call a "fascia", a bundle of sticks of different characteristics; sometimes one is dominant, sometimes another. He could be very kind and very generous, but people didn't generally know that. He hid that light under a bushel. He was extremely thoughtful towards the "disadvantaged" to use a modern term, the people for whom things didn't go well, the rank and file.

When he took control of his father's business he was appalled at the level of salaries his father was paying. He knew his father would never agree to his paying people what they were really worth, so he raised the salaries and kept two sets of books, one which was the true set and the other which was kept for his father to look at. He knew that if his father ever found out, he would take away all his authority, as he had done in the past.

Spedan wanted to leave something behind him. He didn't want it to be a Rockefeller Foundation or a Nuffield Foundation or a Wolfson Foundation, which would merely mean making money and then giving it away. Still less did he want to give it to the state; nor did he want to benefit either himself or his family by putting the money into property and then forgetting about it. He saw how much greater might be the end result if the money was ploughed back into the business. He didn't think a lot of money was good for anybody. He used to say: "You can't sleep in more than one bed at a time, and once you've got three motor cars what do you want any more for?" He wanted to make his mark and his reputation in his own way.

It was a vision that inspired him and he sacrificed a lot for it, not least his own family. But he misjudged the extent of his own contribution to this vision, so wholehearted was he. I'm sure he misjudged it, because otherwise he wouldn't have been so bitterly disappointed that it wasn't more successful in his lifetime, and that there was no sign of it being copied. He thought he would blaze a trail that others would be inspired to follow. It didn't happen and he died a bitterly disappointed man.

Did you like him?

I liked him sometimes. I liked certain rods in the bundle, and certain characteristics; I didn't like others. He was a complex chap. I didn't like all aspects of him.

What did you not like about him?

Well, I think really that he should not have sacrificed his family to such an extent. But I enjoyed being with him. I enjoyed arguing with him. It was stimulating and it didn't tire me as it did many other people, who would come back from a day down here [at Leckford] utterly drained and exhausted from the stress of coping with him.

He was, in many people's eyes, particularly the ex-service people, a cad. The extent to which he would press people for their views and opinions of their colleagues, or even their superiors, would really put you on the spot, because he really only wanted confirmation of something he already knew. If you weren't frank with him, so much the worse for you; if you *were* frank with him, it was just as likely that the fellow would be out on his ear and your opinion would be quoted as one of the reasons for the dismissal. People couldn't cope with that.

I found I could cope with it. I discovered quite early on that he was a great admirer of the time-and-motion pioneer, F W Taylor, author of *The Principles of Scientific Management*. Among Taylor's studies was one of managers. He isolated nine qualities highly desirable in managerial and top level jobs: brains, education, special technical or other expertise, energy, honesty, tact, common sense, good health, and so on. He came to the conclusion that if you could get five of these nine qualities in one man, you were lucky, and six or more was virtually impossible. So I would say to Spedan: "This chap is lacking in such and such a respect, but in such and such other ways he's a damn good fellow and you can't have everything." And I'd get away with it.

He used to say his father's favourite saying was "Praise in public, blame in private". Spedan was very chary with his praise and it was nearly always a case of "blame in public". Another saying was: "Keep it simple", and oh, the complications he'd devise! Incredible complications, which would never work.

His favourite saying was "A plant will never flourish if you keep digging up its roots to see how they're getting on". But he was constantly turning things upside down.

It was his own defects that prevented the Partnership showing the success that fundamentally it should have shown. It took off under Sunny, and it's taken off on yet another surge under the present Chairman. Part of the reason that it took off as soon as Spedan retired was that we'd had to spend too much of our time coping with him and his disturbances rather than getting on with the job. Once he'd gone, it made all the difference. We were then able to do what he'd been preaching over the years – and so often and so signally failing to practise.

J T Webster

Jack Webster, one of the Partnership's gifted sportsmen, worked as the Founder's personal assistant from 1934 until 1941. After war service in the Navy, he spent 20 years in the Department of Personnel before becoming Secretary of Brownsea Castle in 1965. His wife, known as Midge, worked for the Partnership for many years. They retired to live in Longstock where he was for a time the President of the Leckford Branch Council. Mrs Webster died in 1984.

Can you recollect what happened the first time you met Spedan Lewis?

Yes. He was quite severe. He didn't take to me at all. I'd been ship-building and had lost my job. A friend of mine–the rugger player Geoff Conway–had apparently said to Spedan: "Have a look at Webster. See if you would like him." And he really didn't like me. I suppose to that extent I didn't take to him very much, but I stood up to him and, much to my surprise, he appointed me.

Where did the interview take place?

In the John Lewis restaurant.

What did he ask you?

What I'd been doing and how much I was paid. When I told him, he said: "That's pretty miserable". I said: "Look, ship-building isn't a highly paid occupation" and he sort of "hmmphed".

What job did he give you first of all?

I wasn't really given a job. I was given two months in Peter Jones on the selling staff, just to get used to it. After two months there I was put into the West House as a sort of boss–there were four of us. Then one day, after I suppose about a year, I was summoned down to stay at Leckford. We played golf and at the end of the round he said: "I think you ought to go back to the job you came from". I said: "I can't do that, because it isn't there." He snorted at that and I thought "Well, that's that". About half an hour later, while we were having tea, he said: "Would you like to be my personal assistant?" I said "Yes" and started work the next morning.

Wasn't it surprising to be almost sacked one minute and made his personal assistant the next?

Absolutely incredible. After about a year and a half with Spedan he decided to give someone else my job, so I was made Credit Manager at Peter Jones. The other chap turned out to be hopeless, so I was brought back. I think I had about seven years of it.

What was the nature of your work?

Early on I did all the interviewing, but then he began to go

down to Leckford and I did the paperwork. I went down one day a week in the period just before the war.

Was he a good sportsman?

He had been a good boxer at school. He played golf but not very well, and he didn't like it if he wasn't winning.

I don't honestly think he enjoyed his games very much. He didn't like losing at anything. One would have liked to see him go out and do battle with somebody, but he didn't. He always kept to himself, in work and in everything.

I'm told that he could be very kind.

He *was* kind; he was always doing good turns for people. But he could also be very fierce. I remember one person who came out of an interview with him saying "I had a lovely time". The next day she got a note sacking her, so it was hard to tell.

Did many people stand up to him?

I think they did, but not in a virulent way. They could disagree with him but they didn't have great rows or anything like that.

Do you think he got the best out of people?

Yes, I think he did, because the people he'd got worked among themselves and did what he wanted, but not at his behest. I was working up in London and I reckoned that if I saw any difficulty coming from him, I would explain the situation to them and they would accept it.

I understand that people used to phone you up to see what sort of reception they were going to get when they came down to see him.

Yes, they did. And they also asked me what I thought they should say. Whenever somebody got into trouble or into a disagreement with him, I used to tell them how to get out of it.

Did you go on any of his skiing parties?

Yes. I organised them before the war. We used to go to Switzerland and they were always a great success. Everybody enjoyed them. But he was a poor skier. I took him onto what I thought was a fairly easy run one day and he was beaten. He was very cross with me and more or less said: "You shouldn't do that to me". It was silly of me. I knew at the time that I shouldn't

Right: JSL (on the left) on a
skiing holiday in Switzerland,
December 1909
Opposite: Brownsea Castle,
where Jack Webster was the first
Secretary

do it; it was a delicate game and I was really just showing off.
The skiing in those days, of course, was very slow–there were
no lifts of any sort.

How would you describe him as a human being?

I would say that he was one to himself, as it were, that he wasn't
the normal sort of person one finds in business. He did everything in his own way and I thought it was an extremely good
way. I was very pleased and honoured to be working for him.
I think some people thought it was tough but I liked it–and
I had six or seven years in his personal service. He wanted me
back when I got out of the Navy, but I thought no, I don't want
to do that again. I want to do something else in the Partnership.
He didn't take it badly.

Miss C Lynn

Usually known as "Lynnet", Constance Lynn was one of the trio of indomitable secretaries who worked for Spedan Lewis. The other two were Miss Muriel Elliot, who died in 1982, and Miss Phyllis Kay. Lynnet started as a secretary to Mrs Lewis in 1928 and at various times between then and her retirement in 1961 was close to the Founder and his wife. Her last job, between 1953 and 1961, was secretary and housekeeper at Longstock House, the Founder's home. She now lives in Esher, Surrey, from where she keeps in touch with old colleagues and friends.

Can you remember the first occasion you met Mr Lewis?

Yes. It was in 1928 and I went first for an interview with Mrs Lewis. I was her secretary for five years and I met him at their house in north London, in October or November 1928.

How did he strike you when you first met him?

Oh, I was very junior then–sort of relegated to the basement, as it were. He was always very polite and charming but I didn't have many words with him because I wasn't concerned with him at that time. He took me into the Chairman's office in 1933, after my five years with Mrs Lewis.

What were you doing with Mrs Lewis?

She then was still working with the Partnership, chiefly in Personnel, and I was her personal secretary and housekeeper.

How did it come about that you joined the Chairman? Did he come and ask you?

Yes. His word was law and he said "I want Constance" and so I was transferred. But by that time, of course, we were living down at Leckford. We used to work in London during the week and go to Leckford at the weekends, still working. It was a seven-day-a-week job. We were sometimes expected to work until midnight and produce the answer at the breakfast table. Hours and weekends were nothing to him. And holidays were, in his own words, "plainly inconvenient".

How did you get any rest?

We didn't. Occasionally I was allowed a weekend off and went home. We just grabbed what we could.

How many secretaries did he have?

When I joined the Chairman's office in 1933, he had a woman personal assistant, three secretaries and a filing clerk.

How did you arrange the work?

Fortunately we worked extremely well together, and when we thought one had had enough we went in with our notebook and quietly took over, and kept the rota going.

What was a normal day like?

Nine o'clock at the Chairman's office in Cavendish Square, and

Longstock House

if he was really busy, such as when he was doing the company reports, we would stay till late. I left one night to catch my last train home and there was a terrific row in the morning, when I got up there as early as I could and hadn't typed up all I had.

There were three of you, weren't there? Who were the others?

Miss Phyllis Kay and Miss Muriel Elliott. [Phyl Kay remained almost until he retired in 1955 and Muriel, who died in 1982, stayed with him until he died in 1963.]

You must have given nearly your whole life to him . . .

Well, we did really.

Why?

I think it was the pure magic of the man. He was an absolute genius, no doubt about that. We could have murdered our boss at times, but most people feel like that at some time. And, of course, we had perks, many many perks which most secretaries don't have, like being taught to ride, taught to drive a car, taken to Switzerland, taken to Glyndebourne. Even when he took people out to dinner he usually had a secretary with him. So life covered a very large field and I shall be ever grateful for the education I got with him.

It sounds as if he generated a lot of excitement about him.

The drawing room at Longstock

Oh, he did, yes. His knowledge was spread so wide. He could talk on any subject with authority, and he had the most interesting friends, all of whom we met in due course.

How did he manage to make people so loyal to him when he demanded so much from them?

Well, he did. But then, the ones that weren't willing to do that fell by the wayside. It was the survival of the fittest. He demanded loyalty and one was ready to give one's chief loyalty.

How many years did you work for him?

I worked for Mr Lewis in the Chairman's office from 1933 to 1936, when he himself transferred me to Mr Watkins (as he was then) when Mr Lewis appointed him Director of Trading. From 1936 to 1953 I worked for Sir Metford, Sir Bernard and at Odney.

I returned to work for Mr Lewis in 1953 to be secretary and housekeeper at Longstock House after Mrs Lewis died. I remained there until I retired in 1961 when Mr Lewis left Longstock House and moved to The Burrow. [By 1953 Mr Lewis was working almost entirely at Longstock and his secretaries lived in the house as part of the family.]

Looking back across the years he seemed to live almost like a prime minister–always publicly.

Well, that's not far from the truth. He was really rather like that. But he did mellow, may I say, in his later years, and after Mrs Lewis died, Phyllis and Muriel and I got to know him extremely well. Phyl left when I took over as housekeeper at Longstock House. He was very kind to us in later years and when Phyllis left, Muriel and I were the only two there. I combined secretarial work with running the house. His work dropped off after Sir Bernard took over as Chairman, and we used to spend a lot of time in the gardens and water garden. He would still dictate when he felt like it, but life was much easier in many ways. He led the life of a quiet old gentleman.

How did he keep track of what was going on when he poured out so many memoranda?

Well, he had that kind of mind. He had a wonderful memory; he would know what he wrote six years ago.

The thing that's very hard to get at is the private man. He seemed to be always surrounded by an entourage of people; he never seemed to be alone.

Yes, I think that's true, and it must have been a great worry to Mrs Lewis.

What happened at Christmas? Did you go away?

Oh no, we had Christmas at Longstock House, with all the trimmings–enormous Christmas trees, presents in the hall, and so on.

What are your last memories of him?

As a very kindly gentleman. He was still very handsome, although he grew his beard and looked quite different.

You must look back with a lot of happiness?

Oh indeed. I suppose with old age, and looking back on life, you forget the hard times and remember the pleasant ones, but I certainly have had most happy times in the Partnership, times I wouldn't have missed for anything, and a great deal of pleasure–going abroad with him, sharing in all the good things as well as the bad.

Mrs E Locket

As Miss Rosser, Enid Locket joined the Partnership in 1933 having been one of the first women called to the Bar. She was the Partnership's Legal Adviser from 1933 until 1955. She worked closely with the Founder on the Second Trust Settlement and the legal framework of the Partnership's ultimate control. She and her husband, Mr G H Locket, lived after retirement on the Leckford Estate where she was the Branch Council President. She died in December 1980.

The extract is taken from her memoirs and is reproduced by kind permission of her family.

I had got to know Mrs Spedan Lewis quite well in a superficial way as a fellow member of the London Committee of the Oxford Society, and she told me that she was vice-chairman of her husband's business in Oxford Street, the John Lewis shop. She told me a bit about his, then regarded as curious, ideas about how a modern business should be run. It was all quite interesting and we used to chat about woman's work generally.

When I returned from abroad I met Mrs Lewis about something or other and she eventually invited me to meet her husband at lunch at the Langham Hotel where they kept a permanent suite as their London headquarters.

I left that luncheon party with my host who walked me round and round Cavendish Square dressed in a black morning coat and striped trousers, a stiff white shirt, an old red silk scarf round his neck, which he told me had belonged to his father, and talked, as only he could talk with inspired enthusiasm of the Periclean state he was building in his draper's shop in Oxford Street. He talked of the biological basis of his ideas and his dreams of finding the answer to economic problems by common ownership of business between workers and management and the John Lewis Partnership which he had founded in 1929.

He asked me to join it (to help the revision of its Constitution) and I accepted after much thought and discussion with various friends.

The next few years laid the foundations of the most significant and rewarding part of my working life. I was asked by many friends why I was joining the drapery trade when all my interests were in the law. The answer was that I was not joining the drapery trade so much as joining John Spedan Lewis.

He offered me complete independence from authority, six weeks' holiday a year and no definite hours of work. In other words I was to be master of my own time, free to come and go as I thought fit, as long as I did my work. This promise was never broken over all the years.

He was a very remarkable man and believed firmly in giving people enough rope to hang themselves. Many did, as they did not appreciate the man they were working for, a strong individualist who realised that in the sort of team he wanted, personal idiosyncrasies were to be encouraged and tolerated.

When I joined in 1933 I knew that I would find more than a sprinkling of university men and women in the organisation, for I had been told by Mrs Lewis that her husband, as early

Mrs S B M Lewis, from an album of portraits taken on 31 October 1934

as 1920, had started employing university graduates and was a pioneer in this experiment of attracting the educated into trade. Mrs Lewis herself had joined Peter Jones after the end of the first war in such a capacity. She had been at Somerville until the outbreak of the 1914 war and had been recommended to Mr Lewis as a suitable candidate when he asked that college to help him recruit women graduates. She had started as a learner and was promoted to buying shoes, a job she held until she married him in 1923.

Spedan Lewis was a most knowledgeable botanist, but he was also a collector of semi-precious stones, a lover of classical music, opera and the theatre, a voracious reader, and possessed a remarkable memory. He played golf, tennis and rode horses. He was in short a man of many parts and a lover of life in all its aspects. He was a man of deep affections but a supreme egoist, and a curious mixture of determined aggressive forcefulness together with a respect for other people's idiosyncracies and opinions. He could be utterly ruthless but he had the most beautiful manners. He was completely without a sense of class and loved his home which was comfortable but not luxurious, bearing in mind the riches which he possessed. He demanded, and got, devoted service from those who formed his innermost circle. His secretaries, three resident, were driven mercilessly but they never left him. He dictated endlessly except when he was asleep. When he was in his bath a secretary frequently took notes from outside. He could talk endlessly and he once said that he loved the sound of his own voice; and a beautiful voice it was.

I remained, until his death in 1963, perhaps his closest friend and colleague. With most people he had violent quarrels but in all those years I never once crossed swords with him. He had profound respect for the expert and I was his legal "expert". He also liked working with women and I very soon learned that however astonishing his suggestions were, my job was not to dismiss them out of hand but to see if and how they could be made effective. Few of them were not possible. There were times when his ideas were beyond the wit of lawyers but this he accepted provided cogent reasons were produced—and they had to be cogent, for his mind was acute, his memory long and he himself could, had he so desired, have made a great name for himself in that profession.

He had a gift for words but a somewhat involved, apparently tortuous, literary style with very long sentences. He liked drafting papers and often I had the desire to tear them up and start afresh, as did other lawyers who saw them, but we usually found that his drafts expressed when he wanted to say and could not in fact be bettered.

Today, workers in industry are demanding more say in the management of industry, but when Spedan Lewis instituted his notions they were a revolutionary conception of business management and regarded as a peculiar whim of his and slightly cracked and critics said it would never work and that it was not genuine.

I am not going to defend all his actions and the readiness with which he would part with able people but I quite appreciated his motives and I can remember no case where he had not cogent reasons.

To me one of the great charms of working with Spedan was that to every problem you had to apply the same intellectual principles, be it in the purchase of a new business or property, the prosecution of offenders or shoplifters or a complaint by a customer, if only about a packet of pins. His integrity was absolute and compromise just to save trouble unthinkable.

G H Locket

Ted Locket is a natural scientist and was for many years a house master at Harrow. In 1944 he married Miss Enid Rosser, the Partnership's Legal Adviser, and met the Founder. Their common interest in natural science – Mr Locket is an expert on spiders – developed a friendship. Mr Locket now lives in retirement near Axbridge in Somerset.

Personal memories of Spedan Lewis begin in the autumn of 1944, when we were invited for the weekend to Leckford Abbas, where the Lewis family then lived. In spite of having been told a great deal about Spedan, it was very difficult to form a mental picture of the man himself.

We arrived some time before dinner and he was dictating to the last minute, while we all donned, in spite of the wartime, full evening dress. The memory of that first meeting is still vivid. Never had I met a human being with such vitality. I remember still seeing the set of his jaw, and that intense direct look, and his eyes. We went in to dinner, the Chairman–as he was at that time–and Mrs Lewis and the three resident secretaries, and ourselves. The atmosphere was heavily paternal and the conversation not general but directed from the chair, which is not to say that Mrs Lewis was anything other than the wonderful hostess she always was.

Somehow the occasion was not gloomy and suppressed, in spite of the paternalism. Later, with brandy and cigar, I lost my game of chess without dishonour, and he told me things about himself and his family which surprised and delighted me. I had been accepted, clearly.

I never had a business relationship with Spedan. Our common ground was natural history. On a very public occasion towards the end of his life, he began a speech with the words: "I'm first and foremost a naturalist", and went on almost to indicate that, but for the distraction of having founded a Partnership, he would have spent the rest of his life in that field. It is interesting to speculate on whether it could have been so, and how happy he would have been.

He used to tell of how he would have liked to go to some tropical or sub-tropical country and take control over a piece of land and find out as much as possible about everything that lived there, devoting his life to an intensive ecological study. I and others have often wondered if his character would, in fact, have allowed him to do this. Would success have come soon enough? So much of scientific effort results in failure, and though excellence would have been there, victory comes to scientists in rather odd forms, and one may wonder if the abstractions from nature in terms of physics, chemistry and mathematics, would have proved satisfying.

He was, in fact, a naturalist of his time, and the love of creatures or their beauty was very real. I once found him in

JSL with a beetle-net in an olive grove at Menton, April 1904

the upper garden—at that time a beautiful walled garden with box edges to the flower beds—sitting on a shooting stick, quite still, and gazing at an apple tree in full bloom. "It will be gone," he said, "in two days, and its image must last in my mind for the year. We pass these things by too quickly."

It was always interesting to see his efforts to control and possess what he loved so much. He told me how he had once complained to Alfred Ezra, a well known member of the Zoological Society and breeder of exotic birds, that he had no time for watching birds, and Ezra told him that he would have to keep some in captivity. The ordering and planting of a million snowdrops in the woods, the creation of the water garden and the arboretum, as well as the cherry trees in the park, all bear their witness. He loved his orchids in the drawing room, and used to say "Evolution is all very well, but someone had fun creating that flower."

He had a considerable knowledge of plant and animal species, and used to enjoy identifying insects and would tackle quite difficult orders like Diptera as well as moths. Revision of the collections has shown the results to be good, especially considering the time available.

He was always anxious that where he had found pleasure others should find it too. "They should have the cream of all that sort of thing", I once heard him say when talking of Partners and fishing, shooting and golf. It was not surprising therefore that his thoughts turned increasingly in his later days to ways of establishing the study of natural history at Leckford.

He was a splendid and always interesting talker and although he would express a view forcibly, he always respected reasoned argument and expert opinion, and conversation with him on any subject, great or small, was a great pleasure, for with all his emphasis, he was not arrogant. He had a delightful, impish sense of humour and could be gloriously wicked when in the right mood.

The one thing he did not know how to cope with by himself, without Beatrice, was retirement. It is easy to say that in his latter years, say after the war, he should have kept more contact, with men especially, and have rubbed shoulders by joining the Savile, say, or the Athenaeum, and so balance his obsession with the Partnership. But his sacrifice was of his whole self and, in making it, his family joined him. He was a great and devoted man and I was very privileged to be counted his friend.

Right: Snowdrops at Leckford
Opposite: Fruit blossom at
Leckford (above) and (below)
JSL gardening

A Partnership History

Mr John Lewis as a young man. He was just 28 in 1864 when, with fourteen years' experience in the drapery trade, he started his own business at 132 Oxford Street

1836 John Lewis (1836–1928) was born in Shepton Mallet, Somerset. Orphaned by the age of eight, he was brought up by an aunt, Miss Ann Speed. At 14 he became a draper's apprentice locally; by 1856 he was working in Peter Robinson's shop at Oxford Circus in London, and soon became the youngest silk buyer in the capital.

1864 John Lewis opened his own small drapery shop at what was then 132 Oxford Street, London. The first day's takings were 16s 4d (82p), but the business soon grew. He expanded into neighbouring property, and after 20 years, was able to undertake a comprehensive re-building. He called his business John Lewis & Co., but did not register it as a public company and it therefore remained his own property. His trading policy was simple: a wide assortment, low margins, and fair dealing. He never advertised.

1877 Peter Jones (1843–1905) opened a small drapery shop in two houses in the King's Road, London, which also prospered, expanded and was rebuilt in the 1880s. In 1900 he registered it as a public company, Peter Jones Limited, with an annual turnover then of around £180,000.

1884 John Lewis married Miss Eliza Baker. The daughter of a draper in Bristol, she became one of the first women to obtain a university education at Girton College, Cambridge, and before her marriage earned her living as a teacher.

1885 John Spedan Lewis (1885–1963) was born in London on 22 September. The unique name "Spedan" commemorated his father's aunt Ann Speed. At 14 – the age at which his father was apprenticed – he went to Westminster School, and on his 19th birthday he went into his father's shop. Spedan's younger brother Oswald Lewis (1887–1966) also went to Westminster School, and followed Spedan into the family business in 1905.

1886 Shop Hours Regulation Act: the first legislation affecting the hours worked by shop assistants, it provided that young persons under 18 must not be employed for more than 74 hours a week.

1896 Truck Act: unlike the first Truck Act of 1831, this Act applied to shop assistants. As well as making it an offence for their employer to pay wages otherwise than in coin of the realm, the Act protected assistants from unfair fines. The employer could still fine them, but had to make written details available to them of the fines that they might have to pay for breaking his rules, either in the business or in the living-in hostel if there was one.

1899 Seats for Shop Assistants Act (later repealed): this provided that in rooms where goods were actually retailed to the public and where female assistants were employed, at least one seat must be provided for every female assistant, either behind the counter or "in other suitable positions".

1901 John Lewis was elected to the London County Council (Liberal, West Marylebone Division, and elected for a second term in 1904). In return for the support of his staff, he promised to shut his shop on Saturday

Above: Miss Ann Speed who
brought up the orphaned John
Lewis, and after whom the name
'Spedan' was coined
Right: Mrs John Lewis in the
early 1900s, and (below) Spedan
and Oswald Lewis as children,
c 1896. In the school photograph
opposite, Spedan is behind the
shield, second from right, and
Oswald in the middle row, third
from left

The John Lewis Byron football club team, 1907. JSL back row, fourth from right

Grant's House, Westminster School, c 1903

A plan showing the first John Lewis shop in Oxford Street (then numbered 132)

John Lewis Oxford Street, c 1885, before the 1890s rebuilding

afternoons. From 13 July 1901 he joined his Oxford Street competitors in closing on Saturdays at 2 pm; and shortly afterwards his staff were able to form their first sports club, renting a playing field at Acton.

1903   John Lewis spent three weeks in Brixton Prison for contempt of court. He had defied a court order obtained by his ground landlord (the Portland Estate acting for Lord Howard de Walden) who wanted certain Holles Street properties restored from commercial to residential use. They were to clash again over this issue of the power of ground landlords and there was a second court hearing in 1911. John Lewis was found to have libelled Lord Howard de Walden technically, but the jury awarded only a farthing's damages. He continued trading and in due course acquired the freehold.

1904   Shop Hours Act: this second Act empowered local authorities to fix the hours at which shops in their area must close for trade. (There was still no legislation governing the working hours of adult shop assistants.)

1905   After the death of Peter Jones at the age of 62, John Lewis bought control of Peter Jones Limited.

The 1890s building decorated for the 1937 Coronation

1906 On his 21st birthday Spedan Lewis was given by his father a quarter share in the business of John Lewis, valued at £50,000, which entitled him to a quarter of the profits of the Oxford Street shop, and turned the business into a family partnership. Shortly afterwards he became a director of Peter Jones Limited. His brother Oswald was similarly given a quarter of the capital of the business on his 21st birthday in April 1908. Between them the two young men encouraged the John Lewis staff to take an interest in sports and in 1907 they began a staff magazine, the *Byron Quarterly*. (Lord Byron had been born in a house in Holles Street.)

Spedan became uneasily aware that the three owners – one over 70 and two barely out of school – were enjoying between them an income of about £26,000 p.a. of which £10,000 was assessed as interest payable for John Lewis's invested savings and £16,000 was the residual net profit.

Above: **4 and 6 King's Road, Chelsea, acquired by Mr Peter Jones in 1877; and (below) Peter Jones, c 1899**
Opposite: **Diamond Jubilee decorations, 1897; (inset) Mr Peter Jones**

144

Coincidentally the total wage for the 300 employees was also £16,000 a year. Spedan did not think this was fair.

1909   Spedan Lewis was thrown by his horse on 24 May 1909 while riding through Regent's Park from his home in Hampstead to the Oxford Street shop. One lung was badly injured: he had to have two operations, and was away from work for nearly two years. During this time he bought Grove Farm near Harrow; he went to live there himself, and converted part of the grounds into a country club for the shop staff – a better site than the former rented one in Acton.

During his convalescence Spedan Lewis thought deeply about his own future and the future of the family business he was likely to inherit. He was eager to share profits with his employees and therefore distribute what

Telephone, Mayfair 7711

DIRECTORS
H E BAKER
E BARLING
E R BRADY
J E V CROFTS
M M JACKSON
J. SPEDAN LEWIS (CHAIRMAN)
S B M LEWIS (DEPUTY CHAIRMAN)
O B MILLER
A E PORTER
D A RADERMACHER
P MAY
S A WETHERFIELD

JOHN LEWIS PARTNERSHIP
LIMITED

(LONDON OFFICE OF THE CHAIRMAN)

35, Cavendish Square, W.1.

Mr. J. Spedan Lewis regrets very much that long-range consequences of a riding accident forty years
ago prevent his dictating if effort can be saved by a merely general direction to someone else.

had hitherto been reserves, but could not see how to do this without crippling security or expansion. Then, in an inspiration, he realised that if a business was made into a limited liability company it could finance its own growth, and share its profits, provided that the profits distributed to the employees took the form of shares in the company rather than cash. Each year, some profit could be capitalised and the shares issued to the employees in proportion to their pay. This would preserve the cash for the company but share its ownership in the form of an interest-bearing investment with employees. Provided the shares were non-voting, employees could keep or sell them as they wished without affecting the control of the company. His father's reaction to this suggestion, and the consequent smaller share of retained profits for the family proprietor, was perhaps inevitable: "Who do you suppose would bear the carking cares of business for such a miserable remuneration as this would mean?"

1912 Shops Act: provided for compulsory and fixed meal-times, and for a weekly half-holiday: shops were to close at 1 pm once a week, and let their workers go by 1.30 pm. (John Lewis reported to the Peter Jones shareholders in 1912 that a "serious time" lay ahead: expenses had been increased by other recent legislation introducing employers' liability and national insurance, and now Peter Jones closed at 1 pm instead of 4 pm on Saturday, often its busiest day. "I almost would have preferred to close on Saturday entirely," he told them, "because we have all the expenses going on up till one o'clock and it burdens the day's trade.")

There was, however, still no law governing the length of a shop assistant's working week, though in its early stages this Shops Act had included a proposal to limit the working week to 60 hours excluding meal-times.

23 April 1913 Spedan Lewis took his first annual general meeting of Peter Jones Limited as chairman for the occasion. His father retained control of the ordinary shares in the company. The business was not doing well: no dividend had been paid on the ordinary shares since 1906, and even the preference dividend was now 12 months in arrears. Turnover at £100,000 was only about two-thirds of the peak level reached under Mr Peter Jones.

January 1914 John Lewis handed over the managerial control of the Peter Jones shop to his son Spedan – provided that he worked until 5 pm at the shop in Oxford Street. From this point Spedan Lewis was chairman of Peter Jones Limited and the shop's nominal managing director – free to start putting his ideas of partnership into practice, although in a business that was dying on its feet.

1915 At Peter Jones, Spedan Lewis shortened the working day by an hour, and started a system of "pool" commission, calculated departmentally, to act as an incentive to the selling staff. He also set up the system of staff committees, now known as Committees for Communication, which he had earlier tried at Oxford Street. These were a first manifestation of his partnership principles. Elected representatives of the rank and file regularly met the chairman of the company, in the absence of their managers, and were free to discuss with him whatever they liked – a system still in operation.

April 1916   After a disagreement with his father, Spedan Lewis withdrew from active participation in the John Lewis shop (where he was replaced by his younger brother Oswald) and exchanged his quarter-partnership there for his father's controlling holding in the capital of Peter Jones Limited.

1918   At the annual general meeting of Peter Jones Limited in April Spedan Lewis told the shareholders of his intention to introduce a profit-sharing scheme: "Believe me, in the next 20 or 30 years if you want a really sound industrial concern you will have to admit your employees to a far larger share of the total earnings than before. The days when a lot of shareholders could stay at home doing nothing and take a very large proportion of the earnings of a business are all over . . ."

Meanwhile, he made other changes at Peter Jones. He gave the employees a third week's paid holiday (an innovation for the retail trade of the time); he recruited unusually well-educated people (senior civil servants, for example) for principal management posts; and in March 1918 he started *The Gazette*, published almost every week since, in which he shortly produced the first draft of a written constitution.

In October 1919 he set up a representative staff council (the forerunner of today's Central and Branch Councils). The precursor of today's Committees for Claims (the "Donations Committee") was introduced as a committee of the Staff Council.

Peter Jones's trade had improved following the end of the war; even so, to raise cash for capital expenditure, Spedan was forced to sell his own home at Grove Farm in 1919 and move into a flat. He was so distressed at having lost the staff playing fields there that almost at once he bought new, though smaller, premises for a club in Teddington.

Above: Sloane Square, c 1900
Opposite: A directors' report showing improved profit and an optimistic comment from JSL

PETER JONES LIMITED.

Directors:

JOHN SPEDAN LEWIS (*Chairman*).
AMELIA SPARKES.
CAPT. ERIC W. HALL, B.A. (Oxon).

JAMES STEPHEN.
C. MURRAY LEWIS (*Managing Director*).
P. WHEELOCK, A.C.A.

Auditor:
S. F. CORNISH, F.C.A., 37, Walbrook, E.C.

Secretary:
MISS A. SPARKES.

REPORT OF THE DIRECTORS

To be presented to the Shareholders at the Nineteenth Annual General Meeting to be held at the Company's Premises, 31, Symons Street, Sloane Square, London, S.W. 1, on Friday, 25th April, 1919, at 12 o'clock noon.

THE Directors beg to submit their Report to the Shareholders together with the Profit and Loss Account and Balance Sheet made up to 25th January, 1919.

	£ s. d.	£ s. d.
The Profit on Trading for the period ending January 25th, 1919, is	15,528 5 2	
Add Transfer Fees	4 12 6	
	15,532 17 8	
From this the following amounts have to be deducted :—		
Reserve for Redemption of Leaseholds	865 0 0	
Audit Fee	250 0 0	
Interest on Debentures and Loans	4,977 5 8	
Subsidy to Employees on Service	794 11 5	
		6,886 17 1
Being a Profit for the year of		8,646 0 7
The debit on Profit and Loss Account brought forward was ...		7,451 18 4
Leaving a credit balance to be carried forward of		£1,194 2 3

Against a profit last year of £1,254, these accounts show a profit of £8,646 0s. 7d.

This result should not be considered exceptional or precarious. It is a natural stage in the course, which our affairs have been following for the last few years, and there is no reason to suppose that the years to come will not show a continuance of the steady growth of the last five.

Minor oscillations in particular years, of course, there quite well may be, but, to the best of our judgment, it is likely that the results of nearly every year will constitute a fresh record.

THE GAZETTE

OF PETER JONES, LIMITED,
SLOANE SQUARE, LONDON, S.W.3.

FOR THE PUBLICATION OF FACTS, OPINIONS AND IDEAS OF INTEREST TO ANY ONE WHOSE FORTUNES ARE FOR THE TIME CONNECTED IN SOME DEGREE WITH THOSE OF THE COMPANY.

SATURDAY, MARCH 16TH, 1918.

Our Policy, Rules of Correspondence, etc., are on the last page of this issue.

NOTICE FROM THE MANAGEMENT TO THE COMPANY'S STAFF.

Official Communications to this Paper are equivalent to House Notices, and must be known by every one whom they concern.

TO MY FELLOW-EMPLOYEES OF PETER JONES, LTD.

LADIES AND GENTLEMEN,

The main purpose of this paper you will see in a general way from the paragraphs on the last page, which are intended to appear always, or at least frequently. But I think it may be useful if in this first issue I try to put my ideas with regard to it more fully before you than can be done there.

There can be no doubt that large-scale industry has come to stay. Whatever may be the ultimate economic cause or causes, it is certain that in our own, as in many other occupations, men and women achieve their purpose better, that is to say they get a greater result for any given amount of effort, by working in large teams than by working in small ones. We cannot help seeing that the big factory can produce exactly the same thing cheaper than can the little factory, and that the big shop can likewise beat its little rivals by offering the public greater variety or better value or a combination of both. Some people argue that cheapness is not everything, and that the world might contain more happiness if goods were dearer but more men and women worked " on their own account." I think these people are wrong. I think they fail to see that cheapness is really human liberty : that, if everything were to be had absolutely free of charge, every one would be absolutely free, so long, of course, as the law restrained mere bodily strength as it does now ; and that, this being so, cheapness is in itself wholly good and desirable.

Look at it like this :

Suppose 1,000 men, in order to support themselves and their families, have to make 1,000 wardrobes every year. Suppose that each man working by himself must be at work sixteen hours a day, seven days a week all the year through, to finish his one wardrobe. Is that man really free, although he is working in his own home and on his own account ? Is it freedom to be obliged, on pain of starvation, to work sixteen hours every day of the year ?

Now, suppose that those 1,000 men combine into one team and become each of them a specialist in one or two of all the different jobs that go to the making of a wardrobe, and use in one factory such machinery as cannot

The first Gazette, 1918, and
(right) some recent issues

THE GAZETTE

OF PETER JONES, LIMITED,
SLOANE SQUARE, LONDON, S.W.3.

Official Communications to this Paper are equivalent to House Notices, and must be known by every one whom they concern.

Vol. III. No. XLIII.   SATURDAY, FEBRUARY 7th, 1920.

CONTENTS

The Gazette can be supplied to a limited number of Subscribers outside the Company's Staff. Subscriptions must be paid in advance and at least four weeks at a time, each issue threepence post free. Contributions from such Subscribers—especially of a critical and interrogatory character—will be very welcome.—EDITOR.

Extra copies of the current or of previous issues will be supplied, so far as they are available, at threepence each.

Partners and Employees

It is proposed to refer in future to those Members of the Staff who are in the Profit Sharing as " Partners " and to the others as " Employees." This is strictly accurate and seems better than calling people employees who in the ordinary sense of the word are not employees.

On Reporting: To the Leaders of the House

It is of great importance to our prosperity that you should grasp how important a function it is of your own that you should develop and sustain in those who report to you and through them in those who report to them, intelligence, good judgment, and industry in making those reports, the possible value of which very few of us at present comprehend. In a large organisation reports correspond exactly to the nervous system of a living organism.

Everybody knows that the more delicate and perfect the communications between all parts of a living body and its brain the greater the efficiency of that body.

The marvellous batting of Ranjit Sinhji, of which Hirst said that it was not cricket but juggling, was nothing whatever but the exceptional efficiency of the nervous communication of his eye to his brain and his brain to his wrist.

It was the inadequacy of their nervous systems that made possible the supersession of the immensely powerful creatures, of which so many have vanished from the Earth, by new forms of life far less powerful but better equipped in that vital respect.

Preference Share Certificate showing:

No. 826 — Preference Share Certificate — 3 — Shares.

PETER JONES Limited.

Incorporated under the Companies Acts, 1862 to 1898.

CAPITAL £300,000

Divided into 300,000 Shares of £1 each, whereof 260,000 are 7½ per cent. Preference Shares Nos 1 to 260,000 and 40,000 are Ordinary Shares Nos 1 to 40,000.

This is to Certify that Eva Winifred McLain of 32 St Marks Road Windsor is the holder of Three Preference Shares numbered as in margin in the above-named Company, subject to the Memorandum and Articles of Association thereof, and that upon each of the said Shares the full amount of £1 has been paid up.

Given under the Common Seal of the Company, this Thirty-first day of July 1920

The COMMON SEAL of the Company was hereunto affixed in the presence of

S Whitlock — Secretary.

C. Murray Lewis — Directors.

NOTE:—No transfer of any portion of the Shares comprised in this Certificate will be registered until the Certificate has been delivered at the Company's Office.

1920 The Founder's first formal profit-sharing scheme had to be approved by the other outside shareholders, and by the High Court. The first profit-sharing distributions were made in the summer of 1920, in the form of preference shares in Peter Jones Limited. Actually the company's employees already represented about a third of the 1,100 shareholders. From 10 April 1920 *The Gazette* began the tradition of referring to the employees as Partners.

In contrast, this was the year of a strike at John Lewis's shop in Oxford Street, following a campaign by the shop assistants' trade union.

But the euphoria at Peter Jones was shortlived. A national slump heralded trading problems and by Christmas 1920 retrenchment was the watchword there. The slump continued for several years; profits disappeared, and preference dividends for Peter Jones Limited were unpaid. The financial situation was saved in 1924 by a transfusion of cash from John Lewis, whose Oxford Street business rode the storm more safely. The slogan "Never knowingly undersold" was adopted at Peter Jones in 1925 together with the first advertising slogan: "The best value in London and the most obliging staff".

Opposite: The first use of the word 'Partner' to refer to employees within the profit-sharing scheme
Above: A Preference Share certificate, July 1920

153

LONDON'S HAPPY SHOP-GIRL STRIKERS: YESTERDAY'S SCENES IN THE WEST-END.

"All those in favour of a strike, please show." Enthusiastic employees of Messrs. John Lewis and Co., the Oxford-street firm, deciding to "stick together" and "down tools." About 400 of them have ceased work, and they are the cheeriest crowd of strikers London ever saw.—(Daily Sketch.)

Mr. John Lewis, the 82-year-old founder of the firm. He declares that the trouble was caused by the "vapourings of the accursed trade unionists."—(Daily Sketch.)

Fair officials discussing lunch outside a restaurant new expenses for them. All the employees are out except those in the silk department.—(Daily Sketch.)

Mr. Lewis homeward bound after his day behind the silk counter. He denies the allegation that he makes changes in the staff on trivial causes.—(Daily Sketch.)

The laughing throng of girl pickets outside the shop found very little "persuasion" was needed.—(Daily Sketch.)

Smiling girl pickets leaving Morley Hall for the scene of their labours yesterday—outside the shop.—(D.S.)

Driver W. Youngs, who after his engine became a mass of flames, jumped from his engine at Norbury, but resumed duty although badly burned.

WELCOMING HOME TH... room with the F.A. Cup... of the dense crowd at N...

The strike at John Lewis, Daily Sketch, 27 April 1920

1923 Spedan Lewis married Miss Sarah Beatrice Mary Hunter (1890–1953), one of five women graduates whom he had recruited as buyers in 1922. She became deputy chairman of the Partnership, and her name is perpetuated in the "Sabeema" Art Club. They had three children: John, who died as a child (1924–32), and Jill (1927–68) and Edward (born 1929) who both worked briefly in the Partnership after leaving university.

1924 Mrs John Lewis died. The disagreement between Spedan Lewis and his father was now made up, some cash was made available and some co-operation resumed between the family's two department stores.

JSL with John, Jill and Edward

Name... *Miss M. M. Elliott.*

Address... *30. Nicoll Road.*

... *Harlesden. N.W.10.*

MADAM,

SHARE-PROMISE No. 606

I have pleasure in giving you hereby notice that, but for exceptional circumstances, you would have received at this time or sooner *Forty-one*

Shares by way of remuneration supplementary to your normal remuneration in respect of your functions in this business in the trading-year that ended on the *30th January 1926* and that I will give you that number of shares so soon as I can make them available and that in the meantime I will make to you on the first day of June and on the first day of December in each year two equal half-yearly payments at the rate of seven an a-half per cent. (7½%) yearly in lieu of dividend at that rate upon these shares and that, if the Claims Committee of the Staff Council of PETER JONES LIMITED or some other advisers acceptable to myself recommend me so to do but not otherwise, I will consider repurchasing all or part of my capital-obligation under any one of these documents at the rate of twenty shillings at least for one share.

I am sorry that it is impossible that I should define at present with anything like precision the nature of the shares that I shall give eventually in discharge of these undertakings; but I feel that I cannot properly go further than to say that these documents are issued in anticipation of my intended creation of a company which is to control various business enterprises so as to secure their conformity to certain principles, namely, that the gains of any industrial organisation ought to be divided as follows :—

(i). Every contributor of labour of mind or body should receive all but no more than the economic wage of that service or, to express the same thing otherwise, he should receive as a worker for his work the return that he would be willing as a capitalist to give to another person to do for him that same work.

(ii). Every contributor of capital should receive the contemporary economic rent of the use in the particular circumstances of that capital or, to express the same thing otherwise, he should receive as a capitalist the return that he would be willing as a worker to give to another person for that use of that capital.

(iii). All remaining gain, subject to due depreciation of wasting assets and to the provision of proper "reserves," should be proportionate Supplementary Remuneration for all the aforesaid contributors of labour of mind or body.

And that, when this company exists, shares in it having such rights to dividends, etc., as shall seem to me to accord with the spirit of my scheme and of this and of other announcements of my own shall be given to the persons, to whom these documents are addressed, or to their heirs-at-law and, if I or my own heirs-at-law shall decide to create no such company, then this undertaking shall be discharged by the payment of twenty shillings in lieu of each so promised share but up to that time the dividend aforesaid shall be paid.

If you lose this paper, the counterfoil will be probably available, but you should not rely upon that. You should take care of the paper.

I am sorry if much of all this seems to you to be a needless and even tiresome repetition of things that are familiar to you, but I feel that in some cases the whole may be useful.

To prevent any misconception in these regards, I will add that all this arrangement will affect shareholders in PETER JONES LIMITED other than myself in one way only, namely, that it will increase considerably the remuneration of their and my employees to our joint benefit but at my sole cost and that I shall not be myself the poorer by the total value of the shares, that I shall thus give away, but only by that value less the increase in the value of my own holding of shares in PETER JONES LIMITED by that addition to the assets of that company in respect of which this Supplementary Remuneration has arisen or will arise.

I am, Madam,
Yours faithfully,

J. Spedan Lewis

Signed by Mr. J. SPEDAN LEWIS
in my presence,

F. Seabrook Emery

Chartered Accountant,
3. Cambridge Mansions, S.W. 11.

THE CONSTITUTION
OF
THE JOHN LEWIS PARTNERSHIP

CONSISTING OF

ARTICLES
REGULATIONS
MAXIMS AND
NOTES
WITH A PREAMBLE, ETC.

———

FIRST EDITION, 1928

———

This first issue of a Code of Regulations makes no claim to be complete, and will be replaced with the least possible delay by a second revised edition, which it is hoped will be as adequate as possible and correspondingly permanent.

LONDON :
PRINTED BY BONNER & CO. LTD.,
1, 2 & 3, ROLLS PASSAGE AND 38, CURSITOR STREET, E.C.4.
1928.

**Left: A share promise issued in 1926
Above: Title-page of the first edition of
the Constitution, 1928**

1925 Peter Jones's position improved and profit-sharing was resumed. This time Spedan Lewis operated informally and distributed "Share Promises", which he promised to convert into preference shares in due course, and on which in the meantime he himself paid a twice-yearly dividend of $7\frac{1}{2}$ per cent.

1926 Oswald Lewis relinquished to his brother Spedan the share in the Oxford Street shop which he expected to inherit on their father's death. Effectively Spedan became owner-manager at both stores. John Lewis was now 90 and no longer such a force to be reckoned with. Spedan immediately began the introduction of his Chelsea ideas at Oxford Street. The grounds of Cookham, to be known as the Odney Club, were purchased.

1927 Buying and selling functions were separated as a first step towards central buying. The lampstand department at Peter Jones was the first to sell merchandise bought by several buyers.

1928 The Partnership's first printed Constitution was issued in a hardback edition – it ran to 268 pages. John Lewis died, aged 92, leaving Spedan in sole ownership of the two department stores. He immediately snapped up an opportunity to acquire the premises of T J Harries & Co Ltd, the next door drapery business in Oxford Street, which became the John Lewis "East House", just across Holles Street from the original "West House".

T J Harries, 1928

This is a Settlement

made the Eighteenth day of April One thousand nine hundred and twenty-nine BETWEEN JOHN SPEDAN LEWIS of Oxford Street London W. Esquire (hereinafter called " the Settlor ") of the one part and the said JOHN SPEDAN LEWIS, SARAH BEATRICE MARY LEWIS also of Oxford Street aforesaid and CECIL JAMES HERBERT HUNTER of 51 Hampton Road Teddington in the County of Middlesex (hereinafter called " the Trustees " which expression shall include the Trustees or Trustee for the time being hereof) of the other part WHEREAS :

(i) The Settlor is absolutely entitled to Seven hundred thousand fully paid Ordinary Shares of One Pound each in the Capital of John Lewis and Company Limited Eighty three thousand and sixty-six Preference Shares and Thirty-six thousand nine hundred and forty-two Ordinary Shares of One Pound each in the capital of Peter Jones Limited and Six thousand nine hundred and ninety-five Ordinary Shares of the Odney Estate Limited and being desirous of making such provisions as are hereinafter contained for the benefit of the employees of the Trading Companies as hereinafter defined has transferred such shares into the joint names of the Trustees in anticipation of the execution of these presents.

(ii) The Settlor after due consideration has resolved that subject only to the provisions of Clause 15 hereof the Settlement hereby made shall be irrevocable.

(iii) In furtherance of the purposes of these presents the Settlor is about to cause to be registered under the Companies Acts 1908 to 1928 a Company (hereinafter called " the Partnership Company ") under the name of The John Lewis Partnership Limited with a capital of Three hundred and twelve thousand Pounds divided into Three hundred thousand Preferred Ordinary Shares each of One Pound carrying a fixed Cumulative Preferential Dividend at the rate of Seven and one-half per cent. and Twelve thousand Deferred Ordinary Shares each of One Pound limited in

Opposite: The First Trust
Settlement, 1929
Below: The Odney Club,
Cookham

For the first time Spedan raised public money for this in the form of
preference and debenture capital by at last converting the John Lewis firm
into the public company John Lewis and Company Limited, though he
retained all the ordinary capital.

1929 On 18 April 1929 Spedan Lewis signed the First Trust Settlement and, a
few days later, John Lewis Partnership Limited was formed as an integral
part of the scheme to carry out certain of the terms of the settlement. These
were the first steps in the formal creation of the John Lewis Partnership.
By this settlement he transferred to trustees his own shares in John Lewis
Limited, Peter Jones Limited and the Odney Estate. After certain prior
charges had been met, the profits, which would otherwise have been
available for himself, were to pass to the trustees, on certain conditions, for
distribution among employees. One condition was that if the company
required it, any distribution would have to be applied by the employees in
subscribing for fixed interest shares in John Lewis Partnership Limited.

The business was then valued for immediate sale of not less than £1 million.
Following the First Settlement, therefore, the Founder took in exchange
interest-free deferred bonds totalling £1 million repayable out of profits
over 30 years. He retained complete practical control of the business for
an indefinite experimental period mainly through the retention of ordinary
shares in John Lewis Partnership Limited – but he received no further
dividend, fee or salary. In the event he brought the experimental period
to an end 21 years later in 1950 with the Second Trust Settlement:
transferring to the trustees all his remaining shares and his ultimate control.

In 1929 he moved his home to Leckford in Hampshire and made the first
purchases of land towards completion of the Leckford Estate.

1930–1 Start of a medical service in the Partnership.

The original Leckford Abbas (the chimneys were removed in 1979)

Front of the house today

Leckford Abbas (rear view)

Charity Down Farm, Leckford Estate

Jessop & Son, Nottingham, now in the Victoria shopping centre

1933 The Partnership's first expansion and first shops outside London. Acquisition of Jessop and Son of Nottingham (tracing its roots back to a haberdashery and millinery shop founded in 1804), and of Lance and Lance of Weston-super-Mare (another 19th century family business, later closed down after being damaged by bombing during 1939–45 war).

Formal start of central buying.

The Partnership's Legal Department was started : an unusual innovation for all but the largest commercial organisations in the early thirties.

1934 Two more ailing businesses were acquired : Knight and Lee of Southsea (founded in 1887 by take-over of the long-lived family drapery business of Wink & Co trading in Palmerston Road since 1884) which was bombed in 1940 and burned down in 1941, with a new building completed in 1959 ; Tyrrell and Green of Southampton (founded 1898), bombed in November 1940, new building completed 1956.

In 1934 work also started on rebuilding Peter Jones in Sloane Square to its present design ; and on providing the Partnership's first central service and warehouse building in Chelsea, to be known as Clearings.

162

Knight & Lee as it was on acquisition

Clearings service building

Tyrrell and Green, c 1936

Knight & Lee, Southsea

Tyrrell and Green, Southampton

163

Peter Jones, Sloane Square

Under construction, 1935

1935 The old D H Evans building next to the John Lewis West House (part of the same island site) came up for sale when D H Evans moved westwards into its new building. To finance this purchase and expand again along Oxford Street the Partnership raised further preference and debenture capital – this time in another new company, John Lewis Properties Limited.

1937 The Partnership acquired Waitrose Limited (registered 1908), a London-based family business with ten counter-service grocery and provision shops in which 164 employees were doing an annual turnover of £150,000. Mr Waite, who had opened his first shop on Acton Hill with Mr Rose and a Mr Taylor in 1906, was still in charge.

The first use of the name "Jonell(e)" for merchandise made to the Partnership's own high specifications and standards.

1939 At the outbreak of war the Partnership had some 6,000 Partners and an annual turnover of £3 million. It owned two medium-to-large department stores in London and four smaller ones outside, all six supplied from one central service building; it also had ten small food shops and a variety of small manufacturing interests.

The first Waitrose shop at Acton Hill, c 1906

Waitrose publicity material from the 1930s

A 1930s Waitrose pamphlet and two interiors of the same period

How to enjoy STONING RAISINS

WHAT a sticky, messy, time-wasting job is that of stoning raisins !

Housewives detest it ; cooks hate it. Children love it, of course, but sticky little fingers do not stone raisins expertly or economically. And how wonderfully the fruit disappears when Tommy and Doris help with the Christmas Pudding preparations !

No longer need you waste good fruit by stoning it in the old-fashioned way. At the Waitrose New-Style Stores your raisins can be stoned—quite free of charge—by a remarkable machine which can stone forty pounds of raisins in a *minute*.

Think of it ! Your purchase of raisins stoned in a twink in an electrically-driven machine of gleaming aluminium.

The fruit is absolutely untouched by hand, and comes from the machine whole and undamaged—except that the stones have been extracted ! And by how little your pound of raisins has shrunk—approximately 15 ounces of stoned fruit is delivered for every pound of unstoned raisins placed in the machine.

Have your raisins stoned the Waitrose way—we do not mind if they have been purchased elsewhere ; we shall be delighted to stone them for you free of charge.

WAITROSE NEW STYLE STORES

Branches : Gerrard's Cross ; Kensington ; Earl's Court ; Fulham ; Surbiton ; Windsor ; Golder's Green ; Ealing ; Muswell Hill ; Finchley ; Child's Hill ; etc.

Cole Brothers, Sheffield   1940   In January the Partnership doubled its size by acquiring (for £30,000) a controlling interest in the ailing Selfridge Provincial Stores Limited. This company, launched by Gordon Selfridge in 1926, had 15 separate suburban and provincial department stores, 4,000 employees and a turnover of £3.3 million. The following SPS branches are still trading in the Partnership in 1985:

Caleys of Windsor (originally a family dressmaking and haberdashery business dating back to 1824 on its present site).

Cole Brothers of Sheffield (John and Thomas Cole, later joined by their brother Skelton, started a silk mercery business in Fargate in 1847).

George Henry Lee of Liverpool (tracing its roots to Henry Boswell Lee, a dealer in straw plaits for bonnets, who opened a bonnet warehouse in Basnett Street in 1853).

Jones Brothers of Holloway, north London (two Welsh brothers opened their drapery shop in 1867).

Pratts of Streatham in south London (originally a village drapery shop, in

Caleys, Windsor

which George Pratt served his apprenticeship from 1840).

Robert Sayle of Cambridge (Robert Sayle bought the established drapery shop of John Cooch in St Andrew's Street in 1840).

Trewin Brothers of Watford (Arthur Trewin bought the established drapery shop of Mr Matthews in 1880).

Other SPS shops bought in 1940 were Bon Marché of Brixton (closed 1975); Blinkhorns of Gloucester (sold 1953); Buckleys of Harrogate (sold 1953); A H Bull of Reading (sold in 1953 when Heelas was acquired); Holdrons of Peckham (sold 1948); Quin and Axten of Brixton (bombed during the war and closed down); Thomsons of Peterborough (name changed to Robert Sayle Peterborough, burned down in 1956); and John Barnes (closed 1981; the site is now part of a Waitrose supermarket).

To meet the needs of this expansion the single council at the centre was supplemented by local Branch Councils from 1940–3 and local Committees for Communication were set up, with, from 1943, their first full-time chairman.

Trewins before the second world war

Trewin Brothers, Watford

George Henry Lee, c 1953

George Henry Lee, Liverpool

Robert Sayle, Cambridge

Pratts, Streatham, in 1957 and today

Jones Brothers, Holloway

NAZI BOMBS ON WEST END STORES
Oxford-street Struck at Night

OXFORD-STREET was struck by bombs at night, when the throngs of shoppers were far away. This *Daily Mail* picture of London's famous shopping centre was taken looking west. The stores of John Lewis, on the right, Bourne and Hollingsworth, and D. H. Evans were badly damaged, but the basements of these great buildings afforded adequate shelter to many. Oxford-street was barricaded off yesterday.

1940 John Lewis was bombed in September and fire destroyed most of the West House. This large and most profitable section of the Partnership remained out of action for 20 years and was not rebuilt until 1960. Bombs also destroyed the premises of Tyrrell and Green, Knight and Lee and branches in Weston-super-Mare and south London.

Partnership Bonus was not paid, but Spedan proposed a pension scheme.

Taylor and Penton, Addlestone

1941 The Central Council approved a non-contributory pension scheme for virtually all Partners (half pay after 30 years).

1942–5 Acquisition of various small shops, all since sold, including John Pound (leather goods) in London; Bees and Tees, and Schofield and Martin (food shops in the London and Southend areas); and Silk Shop fabric shops in Edinburgh, Hull and Newcastle upon Tyne.

1945 Addlestone site acquired for industrial units producing quilts, bedding and furniture trading under the name of Taylor and Penton.

1946 Spedan Lewis transferred the ownership of his land at Leckford and Longstock to the Partnership to form Leckford Estate Limited.

Below and opposite:
Leckford Estate, Hampshire

1946   For the first time the Central Council chose five Partners to serve as
        directors of the Central Board.

1947   Chronicles began. The first branch Chronicles appeared on 8 February 1947
        at Peter Jones, Clearings and John Barnes; later that year came Chronicles
        at Jessops, Cole Brothers, John Lewis and Bon Marché of Brixton; and
        from February 1949 at Waitrose. The very first branch publication had been
        the *Leckford Gazette*, produced once a month from 1935 onwards by Miss
        Muriel Elliott, one of Spedan Lewis's secretaries.

1948   Experimental overseas expansion: three fabric shops were opened in South
        Africa (Cape Town, Port Elizabeth, Johannesburg) but were closed in 1954.
        Spedan published his book about the principles of the Partnership:
        Partnership For All.

1948–53 No distribution of Partnership Bonus; pay cuts in 1952.

1950 On 26 April Spedan Lewis signed the irrevocable Second Trust Settlement, 21 years after the first one. From that moment, the Partnership has belonged to the people who are employed in it. This settlement embodied the solution to several unusual problems – for example, he wanted to transfer ownership of capital to a body of employees which, strictly speaking, had no legal entity, which was already far larger than the conventional "partnership" of a few individuals, and which was intended to grow larger indefinitely. The solution was to hand over control of the business (the ordinary share capital of John Lewis Partnership Limited) to a corporate trustee. This was a new company, John Lewis Partnership Trust Limited, with the sole function of acting as a trustee. Its directors included the Chairman and Deputy Chairman, and three "Trustees of the Constitution" elected by the Central Council. Spedan Lewis became Chairman of the Trust company and remained Chairman of John Lewis Partnership Limited but exercised all his powers within the Partnership's Constitution.

Spedan indicated his intention of retiring at 70 in 1955 and of nominating Bernard Miller as his successor.

1951 Waitrose Southend was the first branch to be converted to self-service.

John Lewis, Cape Town, 1948

Stamp
10/-
6.6.50

Adjudication
Stamp
6.6.50

This is a Settlement

This is a Settlement made the twenty - sixth day of April, One thousand nine hundred and fifty, BETWEEN JOHN SPEDAN LEWIS of Longstock House, near Stockbridge, in the County of Southampton (hereinafter called " the Settlor ") of the one part and JOHN LEWIS PARTNERSHIP TRUST LIMITED, whose registered office is situate at 13, Holles Street, W.1, in the County of London (hereinafter called " the Trustee," which expression shall where the context so admits include the Trustees or Trustee for the time being of these presents) of the other part.

WHEREAS the Settlor has devoted his life and fortune to an attempt to devise and create a Partnership upon the scale of modern industry, which Partnership should attract, retain and secure the best efforts of persons able and willing to serve the general community honestly and well and should divide as fairly as possible among all those persons for so long as they should be its members all of the legitimate advantages of ownership of its business.

AND WHEREAS the Settlor is absolutely entitled to 12,000 Deferred Ordinary Shares of £1 each (hereinafter called " the Shares ") in John Lewis Partnership Limited (hereinafter called " the Partnership Company ").

AND WHEREAS the Shares now entitle the holder thereof to control the Partnership Company.

AND WHEREAS the Trustee is the Trustee of the 1929 Settlement as hereinafter defined.

AND WHEREAS the Settlor is desirous of providing for the future control of the Partnership Company and has transferred the Shares into the name of the Trustee in anticipation of the execution of these presents.

AND WHEREAS it is intended that the Trustee shall remain as sole Trustee of the 1929 Settlement and of these presents with a view to the Trustee exercising the said control in future.

AND WHEREAS the Settlor after due consideration has resolved that the Settlement hereby made shall be irrevocable.

NOW THIS DEED WITNESSETH and IT IS HEREBY AGREED and DECLARED as follows:—

1. IN this Deed where the context so admits:—

The " 1929 SETTLEMENT " means a Settlement dated the 18th day of April, 1929, and made between John Spedan Lewis of the one part and the said John Spedan Lewis, Sarah Beatrice Mary Lewis and Cecil James Herbert Hunter of the other part in the form in which having regard to any variation thereof the same is for the time being in force.

The Second Trust Settlement, 1950

A self-service leaflet – customers had to be educated in the system

The first self-service Waitrose, 1951

1952   Borval Fabrics Limited formed for the production of woollen dress fabrics.

1953   Acquisition of Herbert Parkinson furnishing fabric weaving mill in Darwen;
and of two large department stores: Bainbridge of Newcastle upon Tyne
(founded in 1841 by Emerson Muschamp Bainbridge) and Heelas of
Reading (John Heelas bought Mr Hutchinson's drapery shop in Minster
Street in 1854). The existing Partnership shop in Reading, A H Bull, was
sold, along with several other uneconomically small SPS branches.

Mrs Spedan Lewis died.

Partnership Bonus restored.

Dornier rapier looms at Herbert Parkinson, c 1978

Right: Bainbridge, Newcastle, in Eldon Square shopping centre Centre: An artist's impression of the new Heelas building in Reading and (below) the existing frontage

1954   Spedan Lewis published *Fairer Shares*, his second book about the Partnership.

1955   Spedan Lewis retired, nominating Mr O B Miller (later Sir Bernard Miller) to succeed him as Chairman. Mr Miller had joined as a graduate learner in 1927 and married another learner, Miss Jessica ffoulkes, whom he first met at the Odney Club. (Her name is perpetuated in *Jeroma*, one of the Sailing Club yachts.) Rebuilding of John Lewis Oxford Street began. First purpose-built Waitrose supermarket opened in Streatham with floor space of 2,000 square feet.

Above: Sir Bernard and Lady Miller, c 1957
Right: JSL at his farewell meeting, 22 September 1955

For some years after the war John Lewis traded from a temporary shop. One section of the store facing Cavendish Square had been rebuilt pre-war, but survived the bombing

John Lewis Oxford Street

1956 The Peterborough department store was destroyed by fire. East House of John Lewis sold, but not vacated until 1960.

1959 Creation of two Directorates of Trading. Waitrose, as the Directorate of Trading, Food, was separated from the department stores for the first time.

1960 Rebuilding of John Lewis Oxford Street was completed on the West House site. The store continued to trade throughout the rebuilding.

1962 The Partnership enabled the National Trust to acquire Brownsea Island and in exchange leased Brownsea Castle from the National Trust. It was first opened to Partners for holidays in 1965.

Acquisition of Bon Marché, the department store adjacent to George Henry Lee in Liverpool, with which it was amalgamated.

Experimental expansion into chain of Ladybird children's wear shops (sold in 1965, except for one in Oxford Street, closed 1977).

John Lewis East (closed, 1960) shown here decorated for the 1937 Coronation
Opposite: Brownsea Island, Poole Harbour

1963   John Spedan Lewis died on 21 February.

New central service building for department stores opened at Stevenage, housing the Partnership's first computer.

Acquisition of Daniel Neal and Sons Limited children's wear business (founded 1837) with seven branches. Those in Bournemouth and Cheltenham traded separately until 1977; the business of the two branches in central London was taken into John Lewis and Peter Jones; and the branches in Birmingham, Bristol and Exeter were sold.

Cole Brothers moved into specially built new premises in Sheffield.

1964   Centenary of Oxford Street business; 50th anniversary of the start of Partnership at Peter Jones; first payment of profit-sharing Bonus (partly) in cash; experiment with five-day working week introduced in department stores following earlier experiments from 1960 in Waitrose, Tyrrell and Green and Robert Sayle.

1965   Acquisition of Stead McAlpin, textile printing works near Carlisle (founded 1835).

The last staff hostel in the Partnership was closed (at Robert Sayle).

Stevenage warehouse and administration building

Stead McAlpin, near Carlisle

The Waitrose warehouse, Bracknell

1968 Central Council Committee set up to examine "sharing of power". Its recommendations were implemented in 1969, leading to some adaptation of the roles of Chairman, Central Board and Central Council.

1970 Weekly communication half-hours reintroduced generally. An earlier version from 1954 in some branches had been discontinued in 1965 when five-day trading began there.

First wholly cash payment of Partnership Bonus.

1971 Decimalisation of currency. New central service building for Waitrose branches came into use at Bracknell; Central Council Committee set up to investigate Branch Councils; its recommendations for improvements were implemented from 1972.

1972 Sir Bernard Miller retired, nominating Peter Lewis as the Partnership's third Chairman. Peter Lewis is the son of Oswald Lewis, and nephew of Spedan.

Jessops moved into new premises in the new Victoria shopping centre in central Nottingham – the first time the Partnership had traded in a shopping centre.

The United Kingdom joined the European Economic Community.

The third Chairmanship begins. In the presence of Sir Bernard Miller and the three Trustees of the Constitution, Mr P T Lewis endorses his acceptance of office as Chairman of the Partnership

1973 The Silk Shop in Edinburgh closed and John Lewis Edinburgh opened – the Partnership's first department store built "from scratch".

1974 Introduction of the first electronic cash registers.

1975 Metric trading began in Partnership stores; Bon Marché in Brixton closed.

1976 John Lewis and Waitrose branches opened in the new Brent Cross shopping centre – the Partnership's first venture into an "out of town" site. Bainbridge moved into new premises in Eldon Square shopping centre – and Silk Shop Newcastle closed. Winter Hill golf course opened at Cookham on land first acquired by the Partnership in 1937.

1977 Waitrose Managing Committee began.

1978 Ambleside Park at Windermere bought for use as a residential amenity centre in the north.

John Lewis Brent Cross

John Lewis Edinburgh

Above and opposite:
Ambleside Park by Windermere
Right: Winter Hill golf course,
Cookham

Opposite: Blakelands
service building and
(below) John Lewis
Milton Keynes

1979   Partnership Bonus 24 per cent.

John Lewis and Waitrose branches opened in the shopping centre at Milton Keynes – the Partnership's first venture in a new city.

Long leave introduced – giving six months' holiday after 25 years' service to celebrate the 50th anniversary of the First Trust Settlement and the formal creation of the Partnership.

1980   Blakelands service building opened.

Below: John Lewis
Bristol

1981   The premises of Lewis's Limited in Bristol, which were acquired in 1980, were re-opened as John Lewis Bristol.

Opposite: John Lewis,
Peterborough and (below) Bonds
of Norwich
Right: John Lewis Welwyn and
(below) Waitrose Green Street
Green

1982   John Lewis and Waitrose branches opened in new Queensgate centre at
        Peterborough. Bonds of Norwich acquired.

1983   Welwyn Department Store acquired. John Lewis Oxford Street celebrated
        £100 million turnover – the year the Partnership reached £1,000 million
        turnover in a year.

1984   John Lewis Welwyn opened as a branch of the Partnership.
        Five weeks' annual holiday introduced for all Partners after three years'
        service.

1985 In this centenary year of its Founder's birth, the John Lewis Partnership has 21 department stores; 78 Waitrose supermarkets (by the end of the year there will be 79, with an opening planned for November); a number of service/warehouse buildings; in textiles a print works, a weaving mill and a converting business; a production unit (kitchen furniture, beds and quilts); a 4,000 acre farm on an estate in Hampshire which also has two residential country houses, a camp, and a golf course; a country club and golf course in Cookham; a residential house in Ambleside; and the use of Brownsea Castle on Brownsea Island in Poole Harbour.

Turnover for the year 1984–5 was £1,206 million. The total number of Partners in March 1985 was 27,069.

Branches of the John Lewis Partnership

DEPARTMENT STORES

Bainbridge
Bonds of Norwich
Caleys
Cole Brothers
George Henry Lee
Heelas
Jessop & Son
John Lewis
John Lewis Brent Cross
John Lewis Bristol
John Lewis Edinburgh

John Lewis Milton Keynes
John Lewis Peterborough
John Lewis Welwyn
Jones Brothers
Knight & Lee
Peter Jones
Pratts
Robert Sayle
Trewin Brothers
Tyrrell and Green

Bainbridge
Eldon Square
Newcastle upon Tyne NE99 1AB
(0632) 325000
Closed Monday
Late shopping Thursday 7.30pm

Bonds of Norwich
All Saints Green
Norwich NR1 3LX
(0603) 660021
Closed Monday
Late shopping Thursday 8pm

Caleys
High Street
Windsor, Berkshire SL4 1LL
(07535) 63241
Closed Monday
Late shopping Thursday 6.30pm

Cole Brothers
Barkers Pool
Sheffield S1 1EP
(0742) 78511
Closed Monday
Late shopping Wednesday 7.30pm

Heelas
Broad Street
Reading RG1 2BB
(0734) 55955
Closed Monday
Late shopping Thursday 7pm

Jessop & Son
Victoria Centre
Nottingham NG1 3QA
(0602) 418282
Closed Monday
Late shopping Wednesday 7.30pm

Knight & Lee
Palmerston Road
Southsea, Hampshire PO5 3QE
(0705) 827511
Closed Monday
Late shopping Thursday 7.30pm

George Henry Lee
Basnett Street
Liverpool L1 1EA
(051) 709 7070
Closed Monday
Late shopping Thursday 7pm

John Lewis Bristol
The Horsefair
Bristol BS1 3LS
(0272) 279100
Closed Monday
Late shopping Thursday 8pm

John Lewis Edinburgh
St James Centre
Edinburgh EH1 3SP
031-556 9121
Closed Monday
Late shopping Thursday 7.30pm

John Lewis Milton Keynes
Central Milton Keynes
Milton Keynes MK9 3EP
(0908) 679171
Closed Monday
Late shopping
Thursday and Friday 8pm

John Lewis Peterborough
Queensgate Centre
Peterborough PE1 1NL
(0733) 44644
Closed Monday
Late shopping Thursday 8pm

John Lewis Welwyn
Welwyn Garden City
Hertfordshire AL8 6TP
(07073) 323456
Closed Monday
Late shopping Friday 7pm

Robert Sayle
St Andrew's Street
Cambridge CB2 3BL
(0223) 61292
Closed Monday
Late shopping Wednesday 7.30pm

Trewin Brothers
Queen's Road
Watford WD1 2LQ
(0923) 44266
Closed Monday
Late shopping Friday 7.30pm

Tyrrell and Green
Above Bar
Southampton SO9 5HU
(0703) 227711
Closed Monday
Late shopping Thursday 7pm

Branches in the London area

John Lewis
Oxford Street
London W1A 1EX
01-629 7711
Early closing Saturday 1pm
Late shopping Thursday 8pm

John Lewis Brent Cross
Brent Cross Shopping Centre
London NW4 3FL
01-202 6535
Monday to Friday 10am-8pm
Saturday 9am-4.30pm

Jones Brothers
340-366 Holloway Road
London N7 6NY
01-607 2727
Closed Monday
Late shopping Wednesday 7.30pm

Peter Jones
Sloane Square
London SW1W 8EL
01-730 3434
Early closing Saturday 1pm
Late shopping Wednesday 7pm

Pratts
210 Streatham High Road
Streatham London SW16 1BD
01-769 4450
Closed Monday
Late shopping Wednesday 7.30pm

Edinburgh
John Lewis

Newcastle upon Tyne
Bainbridge

Liverpool
George Henry Lee

Sheffield
Cole Brothers

Nottingham
Jessop & Son

Norwich
Bonds

Peterborough
John Lewis

Cambridge
Robert Sayle

Milton Keynes
John Lewis

Welwyn Garden City
John Lewis

Windsor
Caleys

Watford
Trewin Brothers

Bristol
John Lewis

Reading
Heelas

London

Southsea
Knight & Lee

Southampton
Tyrrell and Green

WAITROSE SUPERMARKETS

1	Gloucester Road	Oct 37	19	Cowplain	Oct 69	37	Gosport	Jul 73
2	Temple Fortune	Oct 37	20	Kidderminster	Nov 69	38	Weybridge	Oct 73
3	Slough	Sep 58	21	Chesham	Nov 69	39	Leighton Buzzard	Oct 73
4	Chiswick	Sep 59	22	Wokingham	Jan 70	40	Cirencester	Oct 73
5	Dorking	Mar 61	23	Evington	May 70	41	Westbury Park	Nov 73
6	Barnet	Sep 62	24	Allington Park	May 70	42	Daventry	Apr 74
7	Watford	Sep 62	25	Andover	Oct 70	43	Wantage	Sep 74
8	Henley	Feb 65	26	Blaby	Oct 70	44	Crowborough	Oct 74
9	Banstead	Jun 65	27	Lymington	Nov 70	45	Four Oaks	Nov 74
10	Kenton	Sep 65	28	Hall Green	Jun 71	46	Stourbridge	Jul 75
11	Brighton	Mar 66	29	Hayes	Oct 71	47	Dibden	Aug 75
12	Tilehurst	Feb 67	30	Coulsdon	Oct 71	48	Brent Cross	Mar 76
13	Fleet	Oct 68	31	Westbourne	Nov 71	49	Bromley	Oct 76
14	Whetstone	Feb 69	32	Marlow	Aug 72	50	Birch Hill	Oct 76
15	Godalming	Jul 69	33	Wallingford	Oct 72	51	Ramsgate	Jun 77
16	Romsey	Aug 69	34	Horley	Nov 72	52	Marlborough	Sep 77
17	Berkhamsted	Sep 69	35	East Sheen	Mar 73	53	Newmarket	Oct 77
18	Witney	Oct 69	36	Kingsthorpe	Jun 73	54	St Albans	Oct 77

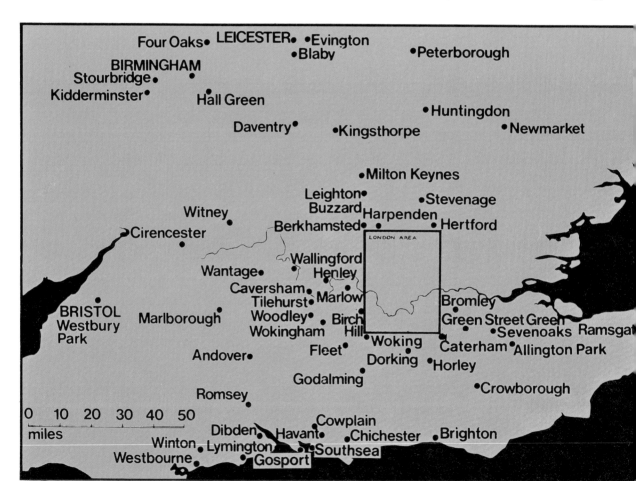

55	Huntingdon	Nov 77	71	Enfield	Nov 82
56	Green Street Green	Feb 78	72	Woodley	May 83
57	Winton	Mar 78	73	Epsom	Oct 83
58	Stevenage	Jul 78	74	Goldsworth Park	Nov 83
59	Southsea	Jul 79	75	Sevenoaks	Nov 83
60	Windsor	Jul 79	76	Harpenden	Oct 84
61	Milton Keynes	Sep 79	77	Caversham	Nov 84
62	Havant	Nov 79	78	Esher	Apr 85
63	Chichester	Nov 80			
64	Finchley Road (John Barnes)	Feb 81			
65	Hertford	Aug 81			
66	King's Road	Nov 81			
67	Peterborough	Mar 82			
68	Cobham	Jul 82			
69	Beaconsfield	Sep 82			
70	Caterham	Nov 82			

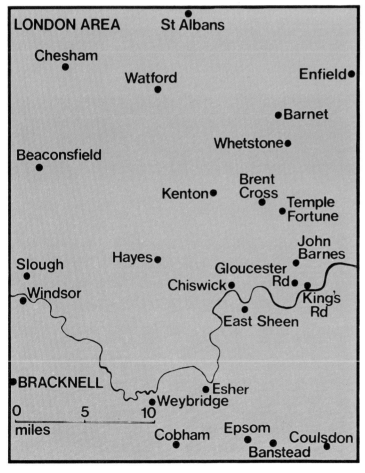

WAREHOUSING

Blakelands
Bracknell
Clearings
Stevenage

PRODUCTION AND RECREATIONAL

Borval Fabrics Limited
Herbert Parkinson
Stead McAlpin
Taylor and Penton
Leckford Estate
Ambleside Park
Brownsea Castle
Odney Club
Winter Hill Golf Club

Biographies

Mrs S B M Lewis was one of the unusual band of women who graduated at Oxford before the first world war. Born Sarah Hunter, she was educated at Winchester High School before graduating in English from Somerville College in 1912. After a short spell teaching she held secretarial posts in several ministries from 1914 until 1921.

She then joined Peter Jones in 1922 and within a year married Spedan Lewis, who made her a director of Peter Jones Limited. Subsequently she became Deputy Chairman of the Partnership and was a director of John Lewis Partnership Limited in the years 1929–51. In addition she was a member of the Appointments Board of London and Oxford Universities, a governor of Andover Grammar School and an executive committee member of the Women's Employment Federation.

She had three children, John (who died as a young boy), Jill and Edward. When she died in 1953, Spedan Lewis paid this touching tribute to her in *The Gazette* of 4 July:

At 6.50 a.m. on Sunday, the 28th June, the Partnership lost in its first Vice-Chairman a very good friend.

Mrs Lewis was always solidly in favour of the sacrifice the plan involved for herself and her children. She constantly encouraged me to put the Partnership first in my own life and she gave to it in every other way, that she could, the benefit of her very great abilities.

During the many years for which stood the arrangement that, if I died, she would hold the Chairmanship, I never had the smallest doubt that in her hands the Partnership would be quite safe. Eventually it seemed desirable that for a time at all events the Chairmanship should pass irrevocably and unconditionally outside our family. To that very substantial extent she would cease to be in her Oxford circle and among feminists, with whom she sympathised, one of the very few women holding in the business world some substantial, leading position. Again as at the outset of our life together Mrs Lewis thought solely of the Partnership's good and agreeing, as she did, that the change was right, supported it wholeheartedly and took in the Partnership's affairs just the same wholehearted interest as before.

There will be a Memorial Service in the church in which she was married, the Church of St Peter and St Paul in Teddington. The date will be announced as soon as it can be settled and will be arranged, if possible, for the convenience of any of her and my partners who may wish to attend. No one should feel called upon to do so from any motive but personal affection.

H E Baker After Brookley County School, Mr Baker went up to Corpus Christi, Cambridge, where he was the College Senior Scholar. He read mathematics and natural science and won the Bishop Green Cup and the Wiltshire Prize, graduating with first-class honours. Initially he seemed destined for an academic life but in 1924 he joined a textile firm in the City of London and remained there until 1930 as buyer and general manager. For four years from 1930 Mr Baker was merchandise manager of Lewis's Limited in Manchester and Birmingham. Mr Baker joined the Partnership in 1934 as General Manager of the West House of John Lewis. In 1935 he became Central Merchandise Adviser and in 1937 Director of Buying.

From 1942 to 1945 Mr Baker served in the Royal Air Force and on his return he resumed the title of Director of Buying until 1946 when he became the first Buyers' Counsellor. In 1949 these posts were superseded by the creation of four Principal Directorates of Buying and Mr Baker was appointed to that of dress and dress materials. In 1952 he transferred to the selling side as Director of Selling until 1960 when, following the reorganisation of the executive management structure, he assumed the role of Director of Trading, Department Stores. He retired on 31 January 1967.

Mr Baker was a director of John Lewis and Company Limited from 1940 to 1967 and a director of John Lewis Partnership Limited from 1948 to 1966.

S Earl From Eton, Mr Earl went to Magdalen College, Oxford. He was a university rowing blue and was in the British Olympic Eight in 1920. He held various commercial posts before joining the Partnership in 1932 as Editor of *The Gazette*. In 1933 he became Acting General Inspector; Chairman of the Finance Committee for Petty Sanctions in 1934; Director of Plant and Stores in 1935; and Assistant Director of Trading in 1937. In 1938 he was appointed Director of Merchandise Research and also acted as General Inspector for a time until 1939 when he became Assistant Director of Selling. From 1941 until 1946 he was Director of Selling until his appointment as Director of Expansion. He resigned in 1947 on the grounds of ill health, but soon afterwards accepted a position at Selfridges, from which he retired in 1965. He died in 1983.

General R E T Hogg Brigadier-General Hogg was educated at the Royal Military Academy, Sandhurst, and commissioned as a Second Lieutenant in the Royal Regiment of Artillery in 1896. In 1898 he was posted to India; in 1901 he was on the Indian Staff Corps of the Central Indian Horse; and served as Assistant Military Secretary to the King in 1911 during the royal tour of India. He served in Gallipoli and France in World War I, being promoted to Bvt Lieutenant-Colonel. He ended his military career as Brigade Commander, Royal Air Force. He was awarded the CMG in 1919.

General Hogg joined the Partnership in 1926 to buy for, and develop, the china and glass department at Peter Jones. From 1930 to 1932 he was General Manager of John Lewis East House and later in 1932 became buyer of furnishing fabrics, John Lewis. Soon afterwards he was buying for Peter Jones as well and by 1934 was a buyer for all the Partnership's branches. In 1944 when the Directorates of Buying were set up he was appointed Director of Buying, furnishing fabrics. He retired in 1947 and died in 1955.

C M Jones Between school and university Mr Jones worked on a farm in Wiltshire which confirmed his interest in farming and his desire to break with his family's traditional connection with the legal profession. At Cambridge, Mr Jones therefore studied agriculture rather than law. He also joined the Officers' Training Corps. When war broke out he was commissioned in the Royal Artillery and posted to Singapore in 1942, where his capture by the Japanese led to work on the infamous "death railway" as a prisoner of war.

Shortly after his return home Mr Jones was offered a job with the Partnership and became General Manager of Leckford Estate in 1945. In 1948 he became Head of Branch at Leckford and Managing Director of the Estate in 1950, the post from which he retired in 1980.

In 1980 Mr Jones was president of the county's Romsey Agricultural Show. He is chairman of the Winchester Diocesan Glebe Committee – concerned with the use of church land. Mr Jones has been a county councillor for several years and in May 1985 was elected chairman of Hampshire County Council.

F T Jones joined the Partnership in 1938 having met the Founder through the Avicultural Society, and came to work in the livestock department which then existed at Peter Jones. In 1939 he served in the Royal Navy and on his return went to the Leckford Estate, where he became curator of the aviaries, the post from which he retired in 1971. He became Trustee of the John Spedan Lewis Trust for the Advancement of Natural Sciences at its inception in 1955. In 1958 he also became a director of Leckford Estate Limited. Mr Jones has a high reputation as a naturalist, particularly in the field of rare birds, and helped Peter Scott in the celebrated Hawaiian Goose breeding project.

O Lewis On leaving Westminster School, Mr Lewis joined his father and elder brother in the family business. After four years, during which he worked largely in the counting house, he went up to Oxford, graduating in law in 1912. He was subsequently called to the Bar in the Middle Temple.

While at Oxford Mr Lewis had joined the University Officers' Training Corps and joined the regular Army just before the first world war as an officer of the Westminster Dragoons. He was invalided out of the Army in 1915 and returned to John Lewis for ten years.

Between 1908 and 1919 he was a member of the Borough Council of St Marylebone and the London County Council.

He left John Lewis to concentrate on his political career, relinquishing to his brother, in 1926, all interests in the business. From 1929 to 1945 he was Conservative member of Parliament for the Colchester division of Essex. He was for many years a member of the House of Commons Estimates Committee, the Public Accounts Committee and various standing and select committees. He frequently acted as chairman of private bill committees.

In 1928 he married Frances Merriman Cooper and they had two children, Diana and Peter. His son became Chairman of the Partnership in 1972. Mr Lewis became a Fellow of the Zoological Society and the Royal Geographical Society and wrote two travel books recalling his own observations on his extensive foreign tours.

In 1951 he returned to the Partnership as Director of Financial Operations–the post from which he retired in 1963. For ten of those years (1952–62) he served as President of the Central Council.

Mr Lewis died in 1966.

M H Lloyd-Davies After taking honours in modern history at St John's College, Oxford, Mr Lloyd-Davies joined the Partnership in 1938 as a graduate learner in the hardware department. He was secretary to the central buyer for carpets from April 1939 until he joined the Army the following November. In 1943 he was promoted to Major and was second-in-command of the First Battalion, the Royal Welch Fusiliers, from 1944 to 1945.

On his return to the Partnership in 1946 he became deputy buyer of men's shoes until he was appointed General Secretary of the Principal Executive Committee two months later. The year 1948 brought the new job of Assistant Director of Maintenance and Expansion which he held simultaneously with the Directorate of Selling in 1949. In 1950 Mr Lloyd-Davies was again General Secretary and was also Chief Registrar from 1952 until 1954. In 1954 he became Director of Personnel, a post he held for 13 years. Subsequently he was Partners' Counsellor (1967); General Inspector (1974); General Editor (1976)–at first as well as being General Inspector; and President of the Central Council (1979).

Mr Lloyd-Davies was a director on the Central Board for 25 years from 1952; and his membership of the Central Council ran from 1950 until his retirement. He was elected a Trustee of the Constitution three times. For many years he was President of the Partnership's Chess Club. Mr Lloyd-Davies retired in 1984.

Mrs E Locket (formerly Miss Rosser) was educated at Oxford and went from university to work at the Lord Chancellor's office. She was later called to the Bar at Lincoln's Inn and practised as a barrister before joining the Partnership in 1933. She was the Partnership's first Legal Adviser and worked closely with the Founder in the preparation of the Second Trust Settlement of 1950. Mrs Locket (she married Mr G H Locket in 1944) made a significant contribution to Spedan Lewis's book *Fairer Shares*.

From 1947 to 1954 she was Chairman of the Partnership's Music Society and was primarily responsible for developing the society's interest in opera.

Mrs Locket retired in 1954 and, in 1958, returned to take up the position of President of the Leckford Branch Council until 1970. She died in December 1980.

G H Locket From Gresham School, Mr Locket went as a scholar to Lincoln College, Oxford, where he read natural science and graduated with a first-class honours degree. In 1924 he went to Arundel School to teach natural science and then moved to Gresham School in 1925. Between 1927 and 1931 Mr Locket was at the Royal College of Science. In 1932 he became a master at Harrow School, teaching natural science, where he remained until his retirement in 1958.

In 1944 Mr Locket married Miss Enid Rosser, the Partnership's Legal Adviser. Through her close association with the Lewis family he met the Founder and was able to share with him an interest in, and enthusiasm for, natural science.

Miss C Lynn joined the Partnership in 1928 as a secretary in the Chairman's office. In 1931 she moved to Longstock House as secretary and housekeeper, where she remained until 1936 when she became secretary to the Director of Trading, Sir Metford Watkins. In 1942 she returned to Longstock as secretary and housekeeper until 1943 when she became secretary to the Finance Director. During 1945 Miss Lynn acted as assistant to the manager of the department of estimates. In 1946 she was appointed Accountant of the Odney Club where she remained until 1953 when, once more, she went to Longstock as secretary and housekeeper, the post she held until retirement in 1961.

P May was educated at Westminster School and was a King's Scholar at Christ Church, Oxford, whence he graduated with first-class honours in Classics. He met and worked for Spedan Lewis during his time at university. After graduating he went to West Africa in the employ of Lever Brothers Ltd before returning to England to join the Partnership in 1932. In 1934 Mr May became buyer of fancy silks, a post which he held until his war service in the Ministry of Aircraft Production from 1940 to 1945. He returned as Assistant Director of Buying, furnishing fabrics, and held various buying posts until he was appointed Principal Director of Buying, house furnishings, in 1949, having been Second Buyers' Counsellor since 1947.

From 1950 to 1952 Mr May was Financial Adviser and served a second term in this capacity in 1955 having, in the intervening years, worked as Deputy Director of Maintenance and Expansion and Merchandise Treasurer. In 1956 he went to the Directorate of Maintenance and Expansion (later re-named Trading) where he remained until 1960 when he took control of the newly created Directorate of Research and

Expansion. As well as his other responsibilities Mr May became Director of Financial Operations in 1964.

From 1950 to 1970 Mr May was a director of John Lewis Partnership Limited; Chairman of John Lewis Properties Limited 1963–70 and Deputy Chairman of John Lewis Partnership Trust Limited from 1955 to 1970. He was Deputy Chairman of the John Lewis Partnership from 1955 until his retirement in 1970.

Mr May's work outside the Partnership was extensive. He served on the council of the Retail Distributors Association from 1955 to 1970 and was chairman in 1958. He was a member of the executive committee of the Land Settlement Association in 1962. In 1968 he chaired the managing accountancy working party which prepared a booklet for the Economic Development Committee of Distributive Trades. He was awarded the CBE in 1970.

Sir Bernard Miller After Sloane School, Chelsea, Sir Bernard Miller went up to Jesus College, Oxford, to study modern history. He won the Stanhope Prize in 1925 and graduated with first-class honours in 1927. Following an interview with Spedan Lewis, Sir Bernard joined the Partnership in the same year, as a graduate learner. He worked for some months as a salesman in the John Lewis silk department but then became personal assistant to the Founder and combined this task with that of personal assistant to Mr Michael Watkins (later Sir Metford) in 1928 and 1929. From 1930 to 1932 he was a part-time sports buyer. In 1931 and through to 1935 Sir Bernard was Company Secretary. During this period he was also assistant to the Director of Accountancy and Estimates (1932–4) and Finance Controller (1934). He became Director of Estimates in 1935, a post in which he remained for many years (the title changed to Financial Adviser in 1942) but simultaneously served three terms as General Inspector in 1943–5, 1945–61 and 1969–71. In 1950 he was announced as the successor to the first Chairman, and was appointed Deputy Chairman the year after. In 1955 he became Chairman of the Partnership, which position he held until his retirement in 1972.

Sir Bernard served as Clerk to the Central Council from 1927 to 1934. He was a director of John Lewis Partnership Limited from 1935; Deputy Chairman of John Lewis Partnership Trust Limited 1951–5 and Chairman from 1955.

There were numerous public appointments throughout Sir Bernard's time at the Partnership. He served as a member of the Council for Industrial Design (1957–66); a member of the Monopolies Commission (1961); a member of National Economic

Development Council for the Distributive Trades (1964); a member of the governing body of the London Graduate School of Business Studies (1964); and was General Commissioner of Income Tax 1966. He was knighted in 1967.

Sir Bernard won a half-blue in athletics at Oxford. He played cricket, was an excellent skier, and a regular member of the Founder's skiing trips abroad. Sir Bernard took part in the Drama Society's revues and in some more serious plays. His interest in music is evidenced by his membership of the Glyndebourne Festival Society, of which he was chairman (1964-9), and trusteeship of the Glyndebourne Arts Trust. In 1967 he became trustee of the Youth and Music Trust; in 1968 director of Southern Region Opera Company; and in 1969 vice-president of Southern Arts Association. In 1968 he was elected Honorary Fellow of Jesus College, Oxford.

Following his retirement Sir Bernard became chairman of Leckford Estate Ltd until 1977. He also embarked on what almost became a second career in university administration. He was appointed honorary treasurer of Southampton University's council in 1974; and in 1983 was elected for a three year term as one of the two Pro-Chancellors. The university conferred an honorary doctorate of law on him in 1981.

From 1975 to 1982 he was chairman of the Southern Region Royal Society of Arts and from 1976 to 1982 was a member of Council of the Royal Society of Arts. Currently Sir Bernard is vice-president of the Southampton Art Association and chairman of the Southampton Philharmonic Society. He became chairman of Staff Trust – Canada International Ltd (Engineering Group) in 1976 and since 1982 has been senior industrial consultant of the Design Advisory Service at the Design Centre.

Sir Algernon Peyton After leaving Eton Sir Algernon Peyton went to Sandhurst. He served as a Captain in the 11th Hussars during World War I. He returned to civilian life to farm on his own estate. In 1927 he joined the Partnership on a part-time basis as Editor of *The Gazette*, Chairman of the Committee for Claims and adviser to the Odney Estate. Later in the same year he became full-time Goodwill Director. In 1930 he became General Manager of Peter Jones. In 1933 he was first General Inspector and Warden, then Director of Personnel. In 1934 he was Director of Plant and Stores until 1935 when he became General Inspector once more.

Sir Algernon left the Partnership in 1938. He died in 1962.

E A Coad Pryor From Haileybury Mr Coad Pryor went to Cambridge, graduating in natural science. After Cambridge he became a civil servant in the National Physical Laboratory (1913–9) and then moved to the private sector as director of research laboratories for British Glass Industries Ltd and subsequently United Glass Bottle Manufacturers Ltd until 1931.

In 1932 Mr Coad Pryor joined the Partnership as Chief Stock Adviser, becoming Chief Merchandise Adviser in 1933. In 1935 he became Director of Merchandise Research until 1938 when he was appointed as a central buyer of fabrics. In 1939 he took over the General Managership of John Lewis until he moved to Peter Jones in 1941 as General Manager. During 1943 he was involved with war production, outside the Partnership, in the aircraft industry until his return in 1944 as Assistant Financial Adviser. In 1946 he became Assistant General Inspector, the post in which he remained until his death.

Mr Coad Pryor was an active member of the Dramatic Society as actor, producer and composer. He was responsible for the creation of the Partnership's Chess Club.

Mr Coad Pryor died in 1958 in a car accident.

D A Radermacher After being a King's Scholar at Westminster School, Mr Radermacher served as a Lieutenant in the Grenadier Guards from 1918 to 1919. He then went up to Christ Church, Oxford, graduating with honours in modern languages. He worked for a firm importing turpentine from 1922 to 1926, first in England then in Georgia, USA.

In 1927 he joined the Partnership at Peter Jones, moving in 1928 to John Lewis West House as Manager. In 1932 he became Chief Sales Manager of both Houses of John Lewis, returning to Peter Jones in 1934 as Chief Sales Manager (the title later changed to General Manager).

In 1936 a new post, the Directorate of Selling, was set up, and Mr Radermacher was its first holder, which he held concurrently with the General Managership of Peter Jones. In the next few years he moved to Oxford Street and then back to Sloane Square as General Manager until his appointment as Managing Director of John Barnes in 1952, the job from which he retired in 1963.

Active committee and council work was undertaken by Mr Radermacher: member of Central Council 1941–71; member of Central Committee for Claims 1941–5 and later Chairman; Chairman of Advisory War Bonus Committee; member of Partnership Book Committee 1945–6; President John Lewis Branch

Council 1949–51. He continued to be President of the Central Council after his retirement – until 1971. He died in 1981.

T G M Snagge After an education at Eton, Mr Snagge joined Lloyds Bank, then the Union Discount Company, for a short period before spending seven years in India as a representative of a jute merchant. During this period he was a trooper in the Calcutta Light Horse and was attached to the Gurkhas as a Reserve Officer.

Sir Algernon Peyton, the then Director of Personnel and a personal friend, introduced Mr Snagge to John Spedan Lewis. Their meeting led to Mr Snagge's appointment as Divisional Manager in John Lewis in 1933 and Goodwill Secretary for a time. In 1934 he took over the Editorship of *The Gazette* until the war intervened. Mr Snagge served in the Royal Navy throughout the war and was awarded the DSC. On his return to the Partnership in 1945 he joined the Department of Personnel, where he remained until his appointment as Partners' Counsellor in 1952, the post he held until his retirement in 1962.

Throughout his Partnership career, Mr Snagge served as a Central Councillor and sat on many committees. He occupied a central position in the social life of the Partnership with his active participation in Dramatic Society productions and especially as the founder of the Partnership's Sailing Club. He was the club's first Commodore and was made Admiral of the club on his retirement, during which he became a popular columnist in *The Gazette* with his "Letters from Longstock".

It was with great sadness that the Partnership learned of his death on 17 July 1984, shortly after the interview for this centenary book.

Sir Metford Watkins Sir Metford (who was known as Michael Watkins before he was knighted) was educated at Swindon and Cambridge (1919–22), whence he graduated with first-class honours in mathematics. He served as an officer in the Tank Corps during the first world war, and after university was a mathematics master at Westminster School from 1922 until 1926.

He joined the Partnership in September 1926 as Chairman of the Committee for Economy. In 1927 he was appointed Controller of Merchandise Finance, later Finance Controller. In 1931 he became Editor of *The Gazette* and held the post of Director of Research until 1935, when he was appointed Director of Trading (until 1946). Sir Metford was also Director of Financial Operations 1945–50; Financial Adviser

1946–8; and Director of Maintenance and Expansion 1947–50.

From 1928 until his appointment to the Directorate of Trading in 1935 he was Chairman of the Committee for Claims and served as President of the Central Council from 1946 to 1950.

In 1940 Sir Metford was a member of the Industrial and Export Council of the Board of Trade and in 1941 he became Director General of Civilian Clothing, devising and running the utility scheme. He was Chairman of the General Purposes Committee of the Retail Distributors Association from 1938 to 1940 and again from 1942 to 1947. In 1949 he was appointed Chairman of the Council of the Royal College of Art.

He was knighted in the New Year's Honours List of 1947. Sir Metford died in 1950.

J T Webster joined the Partnership in 1953 after a period of working in the ship-building industry. He joined on the selling side but became personal assistant to the Founder from 1934 until 1941, when he began service with the Royal Navy. On his return from the war he became Assistant to the Director of Personnel – a post he held until his appointment as Secretary of Brownsea Castle in 1965. Mr Webster retired from the Partnership in February 1969 but returned in an advisory capacity in October 1969 until 1977 and for some of this time served as President of the Leckford Branch Council.

Index